WWW.CREATIVEBUSINESS.ORG

10 LESSONS TO HELP YOU BUILD A CREATIVE BUSINESS YOUR WAY

CREATIVE BUSINESS

**TOBIAS NIELSÉN • DOMINIC POWER
MARGRÉT SIGRÚN SIGURÐARDÓTTIR**

VOLANTE PUBLISHING

Copyright © 2010
TOBIAS NIELSÉN, DOMINIC POWER
and **MARGRÉT SIGRÚN SIGURÐARDÓTTIR**

Licensed under Creative Commons attribution-non-commercial 2.0.
This means you are free to copy, distribute, display, and perform the work and to make derivative work as long as you give credit to the original author and use it for non-commercial purposes. These conditions can be waived with permission of the copyright holder and are not affected by other rights such as fair use rights, the moral rights of the author and rights other persons may have to the work or the use of it. These terms of licence must be clear when reusing or distributing this work.

Published by **VOLANTE QNB PUBLISHING**
This edition is printed by **TALLINNA RAAMATUTRÜKIKOJA, ESTONIA**
Designed by **HÅKAN LILJEMÄRKER**
ISBN 978-91-978368-2-1

The book is based on a project supported
by the **NORDIC INNOVATION CENTRE**

Web www.volante.se
E-mail info@volante.se

If you want to hire us as speakers,
email speakers@volante.se.

THE AUTHORS WOULD LIKE TO THANK ATLE HAUGE AND JÚLÍA BJARNEY BJÖRNSDÓTTIR FOR CONDUCTING AND WRITING UP THE INTERVIEWS IN NORWAY AND DENMARK, AND FOR CONTRIBUTING TO THE PROJECT IN MANY OTHER WAYS. WE WOULD ALL LIKE TO THANK THE NORDIC INNOVATION CENTRE FOR THEIR HELP AND SUPPORT.

CONTENTS

Introduction	9
10 ways of messing up your business (and your creative idea)	13

AXIOM 1: Think big and stick with your idea, and don't take second best — 15
    CASE: MURLYN MUSIC — 19
    CASE: BJARTUR — 24
    CASE: MORNINGSIDE RECORDS — 27

AXIOM 2: There is no time to waste. I want to start my business as soon as possible — 29
    CASE: STIGEBILEN — 33

AXIOM 3: Only you know your product best — 35
    CASE: DNMARK — 40

AXIOM 4: Keep your eye on the ball: focus on your core product — 43
    CASE: LAZY TOWN AND GLITNIR — 49

AXIOM 5: I want to share my work with as many as possible — 51
    CASE: SWEDEN ROCK — 55

AXIOM 6:	*I should do what is expected of me in business: maximize profit*	**58**
	CASE: ROCKPARTY	**61**
	CASE: TINNA GUNNARSDOTTIR	**65**

AXIOM 7:	*Plans always turn out to be wrong, and I am so busy I don't bother with them since*	**68**
	CASE: ODD MOLLY	**73**
	CASE: COPENHAGEN BOMBAY	**76**

AXIOM 8:	*My product is great, it's unique, it will find its customers*	**79**
	CASE: BONNIER TIDSKRIFTER	**83**
	CASE: CLUTCH MEDIA	**86**
	CASE: NIKITA	**89**

AXIOM 9:	*Never say no*	**93**
	CASE: MR. DESTINY	**98**

AXIOM 10:	*Cash is king*	**101**
	CASE: PAVILION	**107**
	CASE: FUNCOM	**110**

CHAPT. 11:	*The investors' perspective*	**113**

INTRODUCTION

THIS BOOK

This book busts the myth that there is only one, fundamentally uncreative, way of doing business. It's a collection of observations and lessons – what we've learnt while out talking to a bunch of successful and interesting businesses.

The chapters in this book are based on what we learnt through interviews we conducted with owners and managers of creative businesses throughout the Nordic countries. Some of these interviews have been written up as cases and serve as illustrations for the 10 axioms we outline in the book. The cases give an insight into why these aspects are important, at least for these companies and quite possibly you too. Since the people and firms that appear in this book are people and firms, it is obvious that a lot will change for them after this book is published: they may change jobs, retire, get rich, go bankrupt, go fishing, etc. Our point with including these cases is not that the details of each case will always neatly reflect what is happening right now in these firms and people's lives.

Rather, the point is that these cases illustrate the issues central to each chapter: what's important is the lessons to be learnt – not necessarily the facts, figures and names.

The cultural and creative industries are filled with myths about business. In particular there are many that think that creativity is at odds with commercial and business thinking. In this short book we give examples and go through different issues in order to show that there is plenty of room for creativity in business. Moreover, we hope to show that by ensuring your creative endeavour has at least some business building blocks in place, you will be giving yourself a greater opportunity to continue to be creative in the way you want.

We have focused on entrepreneurship and business development issues because we know that for many creative people setting up a company of their own is the best way for them to keep working with what they love.

IS THIS FOR YOU?

Who should read it?
Anyone who is thinking about or in the middle of starting up or investing in a business can learn something from this book. The case studies are however from the cultural and creative industries. People in these sectors are passionate about their work and entrepreneurship is typically a central part of their lifestyle. Moreover, working in industries such as software, fashion and music is extremely competitive and we can learn a lot from those who manage to sustain their businesses in these markets.

Why should you read it?
There are many problems facing all new businesses. The primary problem all businesses face is having an idea to sell. The purpose of this guidebook is not to help you build your ideas – we assume that if you are reading this book you already have an idea of what you want to work with and that you are already pretty skilled and creative in your chosen field.

Rather, the purpose of this guide is to focus on the role of money and finance in growing and sustaining small businesses, especially in the cultural and creative industries. In short, we are interested in giving some advice on growing a small business and in sharing some firms' experiences of financing their activities and planning their financial future.

The reasoning here is that capital and money is a resource that is a crucial foundation for your business. Without this foundation your ideas will most likely remain on the drawing table. After all, how long can anybody be creative without money to cover a little food and water?

10 WAYS TO MESS UP YOUR BUSINESS (AND YOUR CREATIVE IDEA)

In doing research for this book we heard so many things said about how one should run, finance and grow a business. Indeed we noticed that time and time again certain taken-for-granted phrases or axioms were passed out as sound advice. What worried us is that there seemed to be a widespread acceptance of these axioms – even though in many cases they simply do not apply and in some cases may prove counter-productive.

We have structured this book around ten of these axioms. There is a degree of truth in many of the axioms you will meet below. However, blindly follow all of these ten and you have ten ways of potentially messing up your business. Our point then is not to hand out a ten-point checklist. Rather our intention is to question each of these pieces of 'common knowledge' and present some alternatives and lessons from the entrepreneurs and managers we talked to.

The ten sections of this book also touch upon a series of issues that academic research on entrepreneurship commonly points to as key areas where firms stumble and make mistakes. Included in each section you will find short case studies based on our interviews with entrepreneurs or managers.

In the following chapters we assume you do not need help with the creative side of the business. However, without paying attention to the business side it may not matter how creative your idea, fashion, film, design or music is.

So we concentrate on the business side, that is, how to start, run and grow a company. A few of these issues are general for all businesses, whereas others are more specific to the creative industries (such as how to deal with Intellectual Property Rights).

Throughout the following we emphasize certain key issues:

- The importance of financing to your business
- The importance of planning
- The importance of business systems
- The importance of learning from your mistakes (and sometimes your successes)

AXIOM 1:
THINK BIG, STICK WITH YOUR IDEA, AND DON'T TAKE SECOND BEST

LESSONS

- START SMALL, THINK LONG. IT WILL TAKE TIME AND YOU NEED TO BE READY FOR FRUSTRATION, DISAPPOINTMENT, DELAYS, ETC.

- START FROM SOMEWHERE. THEN MODIFY, RECONSIDER, START AGAIN, PERHAPS EVEN START SOMETHING NEW. SUCCESSFUL COMPANIES CONSTANTLY CHANGE AND MODIFY THEIR BUSINESSES.

- NO SUCCESS EXISTS WITHOUT PREVIOUS FAILURE.

IT WILL TAKE TIME

A SUCCESS STORY IS USUALLY A LONG STORY

A success story usually focuses on the success, which is often limited to the most recent part of the story. Success stories are, however, typically long stories that go back decades. The H&M-founder Erling Persson, for instance, tried to sell many things before sticking to clothes. Nokia started as a wood-pulp mill, became a rubber works, and finally became a world-leader in mobile phones. Success stories are as much about failures, thinking small, changing your mind and settling for something different than you first dreamed about.

Even if you don't walk straight, you might come a long way if you keep moving. As you will see in the case presented further below:

- The Danish label Morningside Records started out as a digital music service to artists, but eventually evolved into a record label.

- Bjartur started out as a very small publishing house selling books translated into Icelandic but has since expanded into Norway and Denmark.

- Christian Wåhlberg's career was anything but straight and seldom followed a big plan, but led to the Swedish 'pop factory' Murlyn Music that has provided Madonna and other global pop stars with hits.

As we shall see, all these stories are broken into milestones and break points as well as a long term commitment to taking chances. All these stories underscore the importance of breaking down big goals into small ones; or, if you have no big goal, making sure you have some very definite small goals.

These stories also point to the importance of commitment and long-term dedication. In the cases below the founders' devotion to their companies is obvious. This is important for a variety of reasons: devotion and dedication are seen by others and are very important in the eyes of customers, employees, investors and other useful people such as media and partners.

MANAGE DIFFERENT PHASES

Growing and building sustainable business is like running a marathon. It is pretty easy to register for the race and do the first 100 metres but then things have a tendency to get more difficult.

It is important to understand that the start-up phase is only the first of many. Each of these phases will need thought and attention. Indeed, the focus on start-ups in the economy – with all the schemes to help with start-up loans, incubators, allowances, etc. – can seem a bit unbalanced. What is important in the long run is what happens after that first stage.

Thinking about possible risks and planning for the transition from rapid growth to a steadier pace as the business matures (often three to five years after the start) is vital. It is easy to continue thinking in terms of start-up: constantly looking for new premises, partners, investors, etc. Whilst it is important to keep investing, it is equally important to think small and slow and avoid taking on high costs, employees and production facilities you are not yet ready to pay for.

As Christian Wåhlberg of Murlyn Music points out:

> "It might sound strange, but what you have to do when everything is going terrific is to down-size."

Studies show that if you make it to the fourth year, your business will have a good chance of surviving. But between start-up and year four there are some difficult and risky growing pains. Such risks include:

- You continue to chase turnover, not profit (read more about this in Axiom 8).

- Your first hit/idea, around which your company is built, is losing its power.

- Formalising a business built on initial esprit de corps and excitement feels like a betrayal.

- As the business involves more people a confusion of roles and weakness at the management level can cause problems and alienate employees and customers.

- The need to take in new competences quickly can result in recruiting the 'wrong' outsiders.

Understanding what has happened to others at this stage in your industry is useful, but thinking about and trying to sense the risks you are taking on is equally useful if you are to stay the course.

CASE: MURLYN MUSIC
MUSIC PRODUCTION AND PUBLISHING.
STOCKHOLM, SWEDEN.

A LONG AND WINDING ROAD TOWARDS SUCCESS

Today Murlyn Music is one of the world's most respected music production companies. Murlyn has written or produced songs for artists such as Madonna, Janet Jackson, Céline Dion, Jennifer Lopez and Britney Spears.

But 22 years ago, with hardly any previous experience, everything was at stake. Murlyn's co-founder Christian Wåhlberg was running a record store with two friends. They took out a bank loan of 200,000 Euros in order to promote a compilation they had put together out of a few licensed songs from southern Europe. He loved the animated commercial for the compilation, which was called Party Zone, and launched the first TV campaign ever in Sweden for a record.

> "We needed to sell 40,000 copies to reach break-even. I think we sold 120,000 copies so, for us, the profit was huge", says Christian Wåhlberg.

However, from then to now has been a long and winding road. A success story usually focuses on the most recent part of the story, however, for Christian Wåhlberg and Murlyn Music the story goes back decades and is about failures and restarts as well as hits. Although he has come out well in the end, the choice of "wrong" partners has cost Christian Wåhlberg millions of Euros.

He started 25 years ago at the bottom of the music business, as an assistant in a record store before starting his own store. Although only in his early 20's he reached out to investors and venture capitalists. He did not find anyone who was interested in his record store, but got a bank loan as well as financing from the state-owned SME investor Almi.

"We did not really make a big profit in those years and I was never even close to affording expensive watches or cars. But it was a great life. I worked with my hobby and had my record store and enjoyed life. After a while, however, I felt that I needed new challenges and it was then we started the record company."

After the hit with the Party Zone compilation album, Christian and his partners invested in a rap group called Infinite Mass.

"We decided that if we would release their record," says Christian, "we must not make a cover or product inferior to what regular record companies would have. So we put a lot of money into this record and made a type of music video no one had ever seen before in Sweden. A lot of personal favours were collected at that time."

Looking back on his career hits and misses, Christian says:

"There are a few milestones in life. A few turning-points where you have to have the courage to go ahead with your ideas. This step was really important, but at that time I never thought about the consequences. I was 22, without a family ... it was a situation when it was alright to fail, so I was a bit incautious. But you need to be that. You need to be fearless."

Infinite Mass's record became a big hit and was the first urban music record to be awarded a Swedish Grammy.

"Suddenly we were a player in the Swedish music industry. But we were not prepared for that. There were lots of new opportunities but we did not have any money for them."

The company was too big to remain small, and too small to be big. A few of the big record companies made offers, but they were turned down. With some help from a consultant, Christian and his partners partnered with a German company. Suddenly they had a big office but the new and former owners disagreed on important issues.

> "I felt that our company acted too cowardly. So I made a deal and was able to leave and bring my bands, my artists."

Soon after that, Wåhlberg bumped into the songwriter Anders Bagge.

> "That was the first time I was in contact with production and I noticed how unstructured he worked, but the talent was obvious ... So I asked him, spring 1997, why don't we start a company together. You produce and I sell, and we do it from your basement. He was not really prepared and said, okay but only if I can have my own studio."

But again there was no money, so Christian Wåhlberg went back to the venture capitalists he had once approached with his ideas for a record store. As with the German company, the fact that the partner had money did not necessarily make them a good partner. In fact, the investor and new partner did not actually have any money and had to secretly borrow. Out of 400,000 promised Euros only 100,000 were delivered. Nonetheless the new partner had already gotten a big share of the company. The newly established company, called Murlyn Music, had an amazing start with a few international hits. New deals were made, but new money did not come from the external partner.

> "We had to get rid of him after a while, but that cost one million Euros. We had not asked proper lawyers to write a good ownership agreement."

A good partner was finally found in the venture capital firm Novax and this was a new milestone. It was not so much about the money, but rather their continuous advice: the opportunity to call someone every day and test a new idea.

> "I believe that entrepreneurship needs a dual leadership. Someone in addition to the entrepreneur, who is driven by the idea, can run the numbers, ask questions, set a new diagnosis and, if needed, turn down the idea."

Novax bought 12% of the company to begin with, besides a convertible loan based on a higher valuation of the shares; all in all approximately 3.5 million Euros and eventually 41% of the company. Wåhlberg emphasizes that it was not the money that was most important, but the business and strategy advice from the investor as well as the new board.

Advice was necessary in order to take the next steps. One was about selling the catalogue with copyrights for a number of international hits. Christian Wåhlberg failed in his first attempt despite having an extensive, well-designed and printed business plan.

> "That attracted people who thought we were on the brink of bankruptcy, so we got quite bad offers and withdrew the whole thing," says Wåhlberg. "Next time only two pages of information were presented in a very simple way, and we focused our efforts on the presentation when we had some serious potential buyers."

Analyzing the different phases of his company, Wåhlberg points out the risk of the transition from rapid growth to a more mature, constant trend. It is easy to take on high costs in terms of employees and production facilities. The point is that it is easy to start a company, but difficult to keep going.

Murlyn Music has had to redefine its role in the rapidly changing music industry. Murlyn Music went from a production to a management company, with 5 instead of 20 employees, without losing a single client. It went from "a love-all and serve-all mentality" to a tighter organization where they had transformed their creative employees to small-company owners who had to own or lease their studios.

Wåhlberg concludes, although the road might seem to have been well-planned, it was not grand plans but smaller steps that were important:

> "It has only been about doing it. Instead of having big goals, break them down into small ones. When we first worked towards America, it was not because we had planned to instantly work with Madonna. That came a couple of years later."

CASE: BJARTUR
PUBLISHING HOUSE.
REYKJAVIK, ICELAND; OSLO, NORWAY;
ESPERGÆRDE, DENMARK.

What could an Icelandic book publisher and a fictional farmer possibly have in common, apart from fiction that is? For those of you not acquainted with Iceland's most famous fictional character 'Bjartur of Summerhouses' the question might be irrelevant. Yet the book publishing company Bjartur not only takes its name from the main character of Independent People by Halldor Laxness but also its philosophy: "not owing anything to anyone."

This means that the publishing house has never taken out a bank loan, even if their bank managers have found this strange:

> "The bank manager came up to me when I was in the bank one time, asked if I didn't have a book publishing company, and asked if I didn't need a loan? Don't you want a loan? Why don't you? You never take out any loans here? I told them thanks but no thanks, I know I'm a rather bad bank customer", says Snæbjörn.

In spite of the philosophy of not owing anything to anyone, Snæbjörn claims that it is almost impossible to start a book publishing company without capital to take you through the first two or three years. Yet when he himself started the company alongside his literature studies he had no external financing. He got the capital needed for publishing through doing other jobs alongside the company; claiming that his needs where meagre as he was used to a student life style.

Although he claims he never made a business plan and would

not even know what one looked like, Snæbjörn outlines the plan for the business when it started:

> "We wanted to start small, the idea was to start off with two books, then four the next year and eight the year after that. To grow little by little and that has just about worked out."

In the beginning the company mostly published translations of books that were successful in the country of origin. It then slowly started publishing Icelandic literature, and is now one of the biggest publishers of Icelandic literature in Iceland.

The continuous growth of Bjartur in Iceland was further facilitated by acquiring the rights to Harry Potter: a windfall for any publisher.

> "It is usually the case that only a few titles pay for the whole lot. Maybe 70% of the titles never work, financially, but 30% do and make up for it."

One of the successes in Iceland is a concept called Neon, a line of translations of interesting foreign literature. As this worked well in the small market in Iceland, the idea was to bring this concept to a bigger market.

> "The Danish market is 20 times bigger than the Icelandic, so one should be able to sell at least 10 times the amount sold in Iceland. It would at least be nice to try. Then of course it turns out that the sales of translated books in Denmark is just about the same as it is in Iceland. Maybe slightly greater in Denmark. But in turn, if you get an international bestseller the difference is huge. Then we would be selling hundreds of thousands in Denmark, while a bestseller in Iceland sells only 12,000."

In this respect Dan Brown's books have proved to be important for the company and even if the strategy of the early years was to grow the number of titles published every year the emphasis has shifted and is now more on having a selection of interesting literature mixed with crime novels.

All in all, the original strategy of the company is still in play: To grow, stay independent, not owe anything to anyone, publish good literature. In fact, Snæbjörn thinks of book publishing as an art form, and to make the business side a bit livelier the line between fact and fiction is not always very clear. This is true for the story about how the rights to Dan Brown's work were acquired. The official version includes a swimming pool in Slovenia and meeting the author; the truth involves seeing the title, liking it and negotiations through a literary agent in the USA. Fiction or fact, the company has taken a long-term commitment and lots of successive small steps.

CASE: MORNINGSIDE RECORDS
INDEPENDENT RECORD LABEL.
ÅRHUS, DENMARK.

Most independent record labels start with one band. In this respect Morningside is no different from any other label. Jesper Broderson had some songs, and to get them heard he put a few of them online for people to download. If people liked the songs they could e-mail him and Jesper would print a CD and a cover and mail them. Cost was thus really kept to a minimum; the hosting of the website the biggest one.

From the start Jesper was aware that having more than his own songs on the website would make it more interesting to everybody. That way the website would not only be a band site, but a record label. So this was naturally the next step.

> "For me it was a hobby project, so I had no ambitions of making a record label that would grow big fast, the focus was always to have good bands for years."

When he started the label, Jesper was studying and on a state study grant which covered his living costs, and even as the label has grown and he could allow himself to take some money out of the company, he still kept a job alongside the record label. As the label grew bigger, it got increasingly hard to do all the work himself and this was when Jesper Mejdall entered the picture.

> "He had shown interest in the business side of the label and because it had at that point grown so much already I was looking for somebody to share the work with. I asked if he wanted to participate."

Even though Mejdall also has another job alongside his work on Morningside it was important for Jesper that he was interested in the business side of the label. There is no lack of people who are interested and want to help, but they always want to get involved with the creative stuff, and he wants to do that himself.

Along with Mejdall, Brodersen also has an accountant who does the books and taxes. To begin with he did this work himself but now thinks that getting the accountant is one of the best things he has done. All in all Morningside's finances have been very conservative. The company was started with an overdraft of almost 7,000 Euros, which, as Jesper admits, is peanuts. Yet the 20 year old Jesper took this very seriously and made a business plan, outlining the cost of producing the record, keeping the breakeven point as low as possible, and this as well as the personal guarantee of two people secured him the overdraft.

In spite of the relatively low overdraft, they have been able to keep within its limits. Although Jesper admits that this has at times been difficult. The label can only support one act at a time and if the money runs low they have to wait for it to start to come in again before embarking on the next project. This has been particularly limiting for their work in the UK market, where they have been working with their biggest band, the Figurines. Yet, Jesper seems weary of looking for external funding.

> "No, I have too much work with the everyday work, so that it would take me a lot of time and energy to start going out and maybe looking for people that would invest, so it is probably not going to happen ... And because I hate money. I'm scared of it. It really blocks me."

Although this attitude limits expansion, it keeps the company running in the way *he* has chosen.

AXIOM 2:
THERE IS NO TIME TO WASTE. I WANT TO START MY BUSINESS AS SOON AS POSSIBLE

LESSONS

- GET EXPERIENCE FIRST.

- WORKING FOR ANOTHER COMPANY IN THE INDUSTRY IS A FREE WAY OF LEARNING THE BUSINESS.

- INVESTORS LIKE EXPERIENCE – SO DO CUSTOMERS.

- EVEN IF YOUR EXPERIENCE IS FROM ANOTHER INDUSTRY YOU HAVE PROBABLY LEARNT IMPORTANT LESSONS, FOR EXAMPLE, ABOUT HOW ORGANIZATIONS WORK.

GET A JOB BEFORE CREATING ONE

TRIAL AND ERROR BEFORE SUCCESS

Many successful businesses start out doing something completely different than what they end up doing. For many entrepreneurs the first step is usually trial and error. Equally many entrepreneurs try time and time again to set up businesses in the area they love working with. For a variety of reasons many of these ventures are destined to fail. Perhaps the timing was wrong and the market was not ready or the people involved did not yet know how to run a business.

However, not all businesses arise from the ashes of failed ventures. Many successful small businesses are founded by people who worked hard for someone else before going it alone.

As we shall see later: Michael Ivarsson had years of experience of different parts of the music industry before turning around the music festival Sweden Rock; Terje Røkke worked for years at Norsk Filmstudio before founding his TV and film lighting company Stigebilen; Sarita Christensen and Anders Morgenthaler worked together at Zentropa before they decided to start up on their own and concentrate on the kind of content they were especially interested in.

So before creating a job for yourself consider getting one with someone else first.

Indeed, starting your business by getting a job can have several benefits:

- Your experience of somebody else's business will help you know what to do with your own and help you act faster and more effectively when you start your own.

- You will have a network that will know you and hopefully trust you from day one.

- Your business plan will be more accurate since it will be built upon industry experience. Potential investors will look favourably upon this and will perceive you as having a track record, even if not as an entrepreneur.

– You will earn some money (investment capital) and buy yourself some time to prepare for the start-up phase.

Starting your business with a job is common. The founders of fashion firm Whyred worked for H&M for several years. Co-founder Jonas Clason points out that in addition to the experience, they had the opportunity to collect lots of favours from suppliers, grateful after having gotten important contracts with the giant H&M.

The advantages are more obvious when sticking to the same industry. But there is always something to learn and a business is always a business. Putte Svensson, co-founder of Rockparty, first worked in manufacturing but the lessons from organizing projects dealing with water, electricity and construction have been important in his job as area manager of the Hultsfred rock festivals. As Putte Svensson says, experience of all sorts of types of activities can directly help your new venture:

> "Besides, we all had experience from sport clubs. This experience was important when we organized our association."

START AGAIN

Perhaps your first attempt did not work out as well as you expected?

But at least you have some more experience and can ask yourself: What did I do well? What did I do badly?

Even if the experience does not come from another company or another industry, don't be afraid to regard your first attempt as a lesson learned and move on and start again. Just as people quit jobs they are not happy in, people need to understand when it is time to restructure or wind down firms they are not happy with.

In any case, you should not expect that the road ahead will be smooth and straight. (Read more about this in the next Axiom.) Rather, expect everything to take time and be ready for frustration. Don't forget that you will at least get something important out of it – experience.

Another aspect of industry expertise is that you know what you don't know. This kind of experience will enable you to realize that you have to strengthen capabilities with employees, consultants or partners. (Read more about this in Axiom 3.) Through experience you will learn a little more about what your core competences are: what you are good at and what you really need help with.

Experience will also reveal to you whether you should avoid certain activities. Don't try growing strawberries if you don't have the right soil or enough water. Don't sell fresh juice if other juice companies already have exclusive distribution rights with the most important stores. Don't sell anything if your profit margin is worse than the industry average.

CASE: STIGEBILEN
TV AND FILM LIGHTING.
NORWAY.

Stigebilen is a company that rents out lighting for TV and film production. They have mounted a generator and what is apparently the world's largest lamp (175 kw) onto an old fire truck. The lamp is attached to a turntable ladder and is a very flexible tool for lighting locations.

However, the founder, Terje Røkke, did not start life as an entrepreneur with a fire truck. With an education in electronics he started working with lighting 13 years ago. After his education he worked for five years at Norsk Filmstudio and only after this did he start Stigebilen.

Talking about his time on the job he emphasises how important the networks and connections he made there were, and are, for getting new jobs. Moreover, he picked-up and developed many of the skills his company is based on at Norsk Filmstudio.

Starting a business in lighting is not cost-free and he needed money to start his firm. He is financed through Terra Finans, which is owned by 78 Norwegian savings banks. In his opinion the financing process went relatively smoothly. He developed and presented a traditional business plan, and had a history of revenues from previous projects before he went to the bank where he was warmly received.

The loan he used to finance his firm is similar to other types of bank loans: it was secured against a physical asset. The asset in this case was the vehicle but since vehicles' value quickly diminishes the loan had to be paid back in five years. Lending money to buy cars is something banks do a lot of and he thinks this is why the financing process went so smoothly. Thinking about what assets loans can be secured against is an important part of bank financing.

The business has gone very well, and they now have three trucks and are planning to expand into gyro technique. They are carefully considering getting another truck.

AXIOM 3:
ONLY YOU KNOW YOUR PRODUCT BEST

LESSONS

- FINDING A PARTNER IS MOSTLY ABOUT FINDING THE RIGHT ONE.

- BE CAREFUL ABOUT YOUR CHOICE OF PARTNER, BUT ALSO HAVE THE COURAGE TO GO AHEAD.

- TAKE PRECAUTIONS SO THAT YOU CAN BACK OUT IF THINGS DON'T GO AS EXPECTED.

- THE INVESTOR CAN FUNCTION AS AN ACTIVE PARTNER WHO CAN GUIDE YOU TO THE NEXT LEVELS.

FINDING A PARTNER

WHY TWO (OR MORE) IS BETTER

Most businesses consist of more than one key player.

Why can't you do it by yourself? Of course you can: at least to a certain level and especially if your preference is to create a business that will support your lifestyle and not to grow a company (read more about this choice in Axiom 6).

However, if your goal is to create a growing and sustainable business you might want to think again. It is evident from our study that finding a partner is the key thing many people point to.

So although it is your initial idea and you might know your product really well there are important reasons why you need a partner:

- You will be able to continue to focus better on your core product. Without a partner you have to take care of sales, administration and organization too.

- You don't know everything (who does?). So why not take advice from someone who knows a thing or two about important issues for your business.

- You alone is a 'red flag' for investors and other players in the market. They will ask themselves: What happens if you get ill or just tired? Who will design or create your products then? A partner reduces risk significantly.

THE RIGHT ONE

Finding a partner is very much about finding the right partner. Of course, this is easier said than done, but just knowing this enables you to take precautions.

First, there are a few questions you should ask when choosing a partner:

- Do you share the same visions? Write them down and compare.

- Compatible exit goals? Are you in this awaiting other opportunities, until a good exit opportunity makes it possible to 'cash in' or are you in it 'for life'? Be honest about this.

- How much time and effort will you put into your business? If you will not divide the work load equally, how do you balance that in terms of equity and salary?

- Who will do what? Be clear about expectations of roles in the organization, both at the start and five years from now. Don't be afraid to play with scenarios.

Second, take measures so there are exits for everybody in the partnership if it does not work out, or so you can start easy. For instance, the entrepreneur as well as the investor can have an option to buy or sell back the share if things don't go as planned.

A partnership can also start with a small share and an option to buy more at a fixed price if the cooperation works well. This was the case with Murlyn Music and the venture capital firm Novax (see the case in Axiom 1).

Most important is to have the papers in place. Divorces – just like in private life – are rarely nice processes. Bad shareholder agreements have risked the future of many firms – even very successful ones – and even though the company may go on, lacking proper agreements and contracts can eventually cost the founders money and control.

Third, use the partnership. You are now in the same boat.

Remember that partnership is not only about money. A good venture capital partner can help with both strategic and continuous advice. They can be someone to call upon and test your ideas as well as the source of new ideas.

Successful entrepreneurs in the cultural and creative industries often point to the importance of dual leadership – people who can do the numbers are as important as people who knows the product (e.g. who can do the art). The fashion companies Filippa K and Odd Molly, and the design firm Dnmark illustrate this duality.

- Filippa K during its first years was characterized by the, then married, couple Filippa and Patrik Kihlborg – a partnership between the designer Filippa, and the businessman Patrik.

- Odd Molly had three founders – one working with design, one with storytelling and marketing, one with administration and organization.

- The design company Dnmark found that a new partner and managing director took the company to a new level. The co-founders had struggled to finance the production of the orders they had received when an experienced businessman joined the enterprise and made it possible – thanks to a new bank loan – to move much more quickly.

FINDING AND KEEPING THE TALENT

Partners are not only investors and co-owners. Your first employees are just as likely to be partners in a very close relationship. Finding and keeping talent is of the uppermost importance.

In cultural and creative industries certain talented workers are central to your offering. If you don't found the company with one, hire one. But make sure you can keep her or him. Your workforce – especially the key talents – will be crucial to your business and how potential investors assess it.

Therefore, make sure you are investing in the employees' development (e.g. training and education) and in retaining them. Reward structures need to be designed for them: financial as well as other rewards.

The former CEO of Filippa K, Jan Carl Adelswärd, says it is important to identify what drives people. If it is not financial rewards but 'creative energy', how do you balance that with moving forward in a planned direction? His answer is to define limits as well as goals – thinking inside the box instead of outside of the box. This can be useful, he suggests, since he believes that 'the creative people' like that clarity of purpose which goals entail.

This is also a question about designing good teams. The publishing group Bonnier Tidskrifter, for instance, always establishes a dual management team for their magazines. One editor-in-chief and one marketing director. Furthermore, these people also work with a business controller.

Different stages also need different kinds of competence. A director of a company with ten employees will need another set of capabilities than one with hundred. A small-company director is more operative and works closely with all employees. A large-company director lets other people do the operative work. As Jan Carl Adelswärd at Filippa K says:

"After a while, it is necessary to have a CEO who likes numbers."

CASE: DNMARK
FURNITURE DESIGN AND PRODUCTION.
COPENHAGEN, DENMARK.

Dnmark was launched in 2005 by designer and architect René Hougaard and cabinetmaker and product developer Jens Hornbæk. They met when Jens was working at a bigger Danish furniture company where René came to pitch his designs. Dnmark's concept was based on the idea that the Danish furniture industry was stuck in an intermediate position between a constant demand for the designs of old masters like Arne Jacobsen and a pressure from the market to see something novel from Denmark. Rene and Jens' company Dnmark is based on the philosophy of embracing simple design and functionality but combining it with the latest technology and Danish craftsmanship. This has resulted in products that are one hundred percent Danish design but at a reasonable price.

Of course, selling furniture involves more than a design on paper: prototypes and demonstration models need to be made. To be able to produce the prototype of what became their first hit piece, the Pablo chair, Jens called on his network. He presented the project to potential producers and asked them to believe in the project and share the risk by giving him as low a price as possible. In this way production costs were held to a minimum. Yet funding was still needed and to finance the production of Pablo, Jens and René went to several banks with their business plan. "Banks are banks" was Jens' first response when describing how banks reacted to Dnmarks' first business plan. In total they went to ten different banks which all had different excuses for not wanting to lend them the money needed:

"The thing is that bankers don't understand what we are doing. They basically think we are crazy; because I said no to a monthly salary, a fairly good one, to do a crazy project like this. They would basically say, well you are stupid."

It was a mix of different factors and political circumstances that in the end got them a loan from a bank. At that time it was the government's policy to financially support start-up companies in Denmark. The government had therefore made an agreement with some banks to lower their risk in lending money to start-up companies by paying back 75% of the loan if the start-up company went bankrupt.

Design and prototypes are only the first phase and once orders come in actual pieces (chairs, tables, etc.) have to be produced and shipped: something that can be very capital intensive. Dnmark's first project, the Pablo chair, became a big success and the company grew fast. The money Dnmark had borrowed to get started wasn't enough and to finance the increasing number of orders they were receiving they needed more and more money to produce the furniture. Even though a financial gap between finalising production and getting paid for each order is a constant theme in furniture production these gaps led to struggles with the bank. According to Jens, the bank had put Dnmark on the 'lowest shelf' and they couldn't get higher up to get better loans and more credit. As Jens put it, the bank didn't understand Dnmark's business processes so Jens and René were chasing their own tail, getting more and more orders so the financial gap increased and with this the bank became less and less understanding of their situation. The turning point for Dnmark was getting in contact with a financial adviser, Morten Lund, who soon became their business partner and managing director of the company.

Morten Lund was an experienced business man and it didn't take him a long time to figure out Dnmark's need for a full time employee or a partner that could take care of the business and financial aspects of the fast growing company. Morten became a partner in Dnmark and changed their approach towards the bank, which resulted in moving their business to a new bank with better service. Morten knew how to talk to bank people and as Morten himself said, it was more or less Jens and René's own fault how difficult the communication with their bank had become since they didn't know what to do and how to present their ideas and strategy. As Jens put it:

> "We could not have done it without him, because he knew his way around accounting and lawyers and talking to bank people the right way."

What Morten did is a mix of few things. He was experienced in dealing with banks, hence familiar with the financial environment. According to Morten, it is more important to present a strategy and financial plan to the banks, not necessarily business plans as such, like Jens and René did. The banks needed to get a clear and compelling message about the commercial value of the strategy with an emphasis on prospective returns on their investment. Jens and René know this now and say about their initial business plan:

> "Sometimes we take it out these days for jokes. We had a good idea about what we wanted to do but it was fairly naïve, I would say. Today we have changed from being a design company to being a production company.
> You have to choose which way you want to go. You cannot do both. We tried that for a while but the production company just kind of takes over because you can't run two companies in one, you need to be very specific and put your energy into one place."

AXIOM 4:
KEEP YOUR EYE ON THE BALL: FOCUS ON YOUR CORE PRODUCT

LESSONS

- YOUR CORE PRODUCT IS DEPENDENT ON MARKET FORCES, WHICH ARE CHANGING ALL THE TIME.
- PORTFOLIO STRATEGIES CAN HELP YOU GENERATE SYNERGIES AND SEVERAL REVENUE STREAMS.
- IT IS POSSIBLE TO PRODUCE ONE THING, BUT GET PAID FOR OTHER PRODUCTS.
- EXPANDING THE PRODUCT PORTFOLIO IS NOT THE SAME AS LOSING FOCUS ON WHAT GENERATES BUSINESS.

VALUE AND PRICING

WHAT IS YOUR CORE PRODUCT?

You probably have heard that one about not putting all your eggs in one basket.

There is a reason why you have heard it: It is actually a pretty good piece of advice.

There are several benefits to having more than one basket. In business terms these baskets come in the form of products and revenue streams:

- More products using the same brand name help to build the brand. Brand recognition and brand awareness are basically always a good thing.

- Reducing your risks. If one product fails or stops generating profit, other products can hopefully balance out that loss.

- Increase profits due to synergy effects. For instance, fixed costs such as distribution channels and overheads are already paid for so why not use them for more than one thing.

The key word here is differentiation. You can differentiate with regard to either products or markets, that is, you can either create new products or enter new markets. You can also combine these two elements, for instance current products on new markets or new products in current markets. The table below explains the possibilities.

	PRODUCTS	
	NEW PRODUCTS	CURRENT PRODUCTS
MARKETS — NEW MARKETS		
MARKETS — CURRENT MARKETS		

If you are in music, for instance, your core product is the music but many other things than recorded music can be important revenue streams: e.g. the t-shirts and beer sold at your concerts or the mobile phone ringtone that has very little relation to the track you put your heart and soul into. The two annual rock festivals Sweden Rock and Hultsfred illustrate how organizations concentrating on one core product (a festival) can generate revenue from a host of different add-ons or 'sidelines'.

- Sweden Rock is a successful heavy metal and rock festival that has developed a reputation and brand name the organisers use for a variety of other activities such as an online record store, a restaurant, a magazine, package tourism, and an agency. Such activities need to generate profit but at the same time help to build the brand Sweden Rock and eventually sell more (or more expensive) festival tickets.

- The organisation behind Hultsfred Festival has used its 25 years' experience of organising rock festivals and concerts in many other areas: corporate events, education, youth camps, digital media services, and a restaurant. Some of these activities are in order to make money others are just to do good. Remember, for a not-for-profit association not all activities need to be profitable.

Remember then that expanding the product portfolio is not the same as losing focus on what generates business; even if you may not know what it will be from the beginning.

Acne – the Swedish fashion and design company that is mostly famous for its jeans but also produces toys, films and a magazine as well as operating as an advertising agency – started out as a creative lab doing on the one hand whatever could pay the rent and on the other whatever that was fun.

The company was founded by four people with a background in the advertising industry, three designers and one project manager. The plan was – unlike most advertising and design companies which only work on assignment – to make room and money for experiments.

Acne did design and media work that attracted a lot of attention. They created a synthesizer, a camera and a character named Netbaby they hoped would become more famous than "Hello Kitty." By coincidence, one of the founders, Johnny Johansson, made a few dozens of jeans to give to friends and customers. No one could have guessed that from those jeans a fashion company would spin off and create the foundation of a 40 million Euro company. Nor would one have thought that making a hit in fashion would trigger the collapse of the company in its first form.

The enormous commercial success of the fashion side of Acne made balancing the different sides of the firm difficult. What status should the fashion side be given? Should it eclipse other less successful activities? What about the "art" and experiments? What would finance what? It is fair to say that Acne in its original form did not manage to balance these elements and has now been reorganized. The fashion division is now a separate company, even if the current two companies share a website and office space (a former bank in Stockholm's Old Town) and stand together trying to look like a modern version of Andy Warhol's Factory. Acne even labels itself as 'Art/Industry'.

GET PAID – BUT NOT FOR PRODUCT

Expanding the product portfolio is a question of taking advantage of what you have and what you can do, now and tomorrow. Keeping a focus on the core product or your core competence is vital to your business, but you can use your knowledge, brand, contacts and structures to generate more from the same foundation.

Nevertheless, some products may be good for reasons other than getting paid. For instance, even though it is sold in stores in several countries Acne's magazine Acne Paper is more about PR than generating sales.

Let us get back to the live music business for another example. The lion's share of revenue usually comes from ticket sales but a good second can often come from selling burgers and beers. So does this mean live music organizers are in the restaurant business too? Yes, in the sense that they definitely have to understand the basics of selling food and drinks. The important point, however, is that they make money on this too.

In a few cases, what you make money on is not what you thought you would sell, but what creates value is not always the same as what people will buy. So what really might be your core product? In some cases it may even be a good idea to give your precious 'baby' away for free.

Even for established recording artists it can sometimes be appropriate to give away your tracks for free. For instance, the artist formally known as Prince gave his album 'Planet Earth' away free with the Sunday Edition of London's 'Daily Mail'… which helped him advertise and sell-out a series of concerts in London.

What are called loss-leaders can take many forms and can be central to getting your name into the public imagination or to locking consumers into a long and profitable relationship. This is what Gillette does when they sell their razor sets cheaply but charge heavily for replacement blades. This is what media companies do when they let you watch television or read newspapers for free, but sell adverts which you end up seeing. This is what museums and galleries do when they sell books, coffee and food next to their free or low-priced exhibitions. This is also what Ryanair does when it gives away free plane tickets but charges for checking in extra luggage, priority boarding, airport transfers, seatback advertising space, water, sandwiches etc.

The point is, don't be so sensitive about what you have created. People may love it, but it might be a better idea that they pay for something else. Just figure out what it might be.

CASE: LAZY TOWN AND GLITNIR
LAZY TOWN ENTERTAINMENT.
CROSS MEDIA ENTERTAINMENT PRODUCTION.
GARDABÆR, ICELAND.

For years Icelandic children have been running and dancing around to the cheers and encouragement of the Lazy Town character Sportacus – whilst wearing Lazy Town sneakers and downing Lazy Town health snacks. The man behind this craze, Magnus Scheving, was a well known athlete in Iceland before taking on the role of Sportacus. His inspiration for Lazy Town was a lack of healthy-living role models for kids and Magnus decided that he would to do something about this. He started out with a book, then adapted the book to a theatre play, and from there moved the concept on to other platforms from sporting events, to health food, and banking with an emphasis on saving.

After successfully using Iceland as a test market for eight years and travelling around the world doing market research, talking to his future competitors, and spotting prospective consumers, Magnus came up with a strategy.

Although TV production is at the core of Lazy Town the concept is really built around Lazy Town and its inhabitants and the wide variety of things they might need. Aside from the books and TV show there are products such as clothing, water, board games and toys that encourage movement and other health conscious items. Though the company's core product and intellectual property is in the TV show they can earn money indirectly from the idea behind the TV series. This was very important as the TV production was very ambitious and used the latest technology to combine human actors, animation and puppets to create a vivid background to the health messages. The ambitious standard was very costly and meant that it was important to have other revenue streams than TV rights.

Although Magnus saw the potential of using the concept in a much broader perspective than just the TV series, the financial value of this is still very difficult to estimate as the reception of the spin-off products would very much depend on the reception of the TV series. In this Lazy Town is in the same situation as many if not most creative companies.

Creative companies build their competitive advantage on intellectual property: which is difficult to precisely value. According to Johann Omarsson from Glitnir investment bank this was by far the most difficult thing to evaluate during the financing of Lazy Town. But according to him Magnus gained credibility as he was able to show results from the Icelandic market. That gave the bank a rough idea of the ways the intellectual property might be used to generate income.

> "The evaluation of the intellectual property rights will always just be an estimate. To be able to present some kind of results like Lazy Town was able to do after the test period was therefore one of the crucial elements in the process of gaining finances for the global expansion." (Johann Omarsson)

In 2006 Lazy Town won the BAFTA award as the best international TV program for children and was nominated in 2008. The show (and related products) has been sold to over 100 countries all over the world.

AXIOM 5:
I WANT TO SHARE MY WORK WITH AS MANY AS POSSIBLE

LESSONS

- SHARE YOUR WORK, BUT BE CAREFUL ABOUT PROTECTING AND GETTING PAID FOR IT (AT LEAST IN SOME WAY).

- LICENSING CAN BE POWERFUL: OTHERS PAY FOR EXPLOITING YOUR INTELLECTUAL PROPERTY.

- PIRACY EXISTS IN ALL INDUSTRIES AND YOU NEED TO HAVE A CONSCIOUS STRATEGY FOR EITHER COMBATING IT OR EMBRACING IT: THE CHOICE IS YOURS – BUT DO MAKE A CHOICE.

PROTECTING YOUR IDEAS

CREATIONS OF THE MIND

This is not about you being flattered, getting lots of Google hits or enlightening the world with your products and ideas. Making money is not sharing your work with as many as possible. Making money is about getting paid.

If you want to make money – then ownership is what counts.

The great thing about ownership is that you can make money from it. Controlling your intellectual property means that it can work for you even when you cannot work with it yourself: for instance, you could license your work to a better looking singer or your handbag design to someone who works with leather.

Ownership can come in many forms and one of them is intellectual property (IP). Intellectual property refers to creations of the mind: inventions, literary and artistic works, as well as symbols, names, images, brands, blueprints and designs used in commerce. Intellectual property rights (IPR) is the legal field associated with these creations.

Licensing his work is what Magnus Scheving did with his "Lazy Town." He was careful to protect the sole right to the works and the brand when working with distributors, designers, actors and other subcontractors. This gives him extra revenue from e.g. merchandise, which gives him greater freedom to develop the sides he is most interested in.

Controlling your intellectual property is also planning for the future – you never know when your ideas will come back into fashion, be discovered by a new audience, or what potential new formats or spin-offs might arise.

As we shall see the rock festival "Sweden Rock" has been successfully exploiting its brand outside the live music world. Sweden Rock's former owner Michael Ivarsson says that ultimately his main job was not arranging rock festivals but building and making money from the brand.

"We shall not do everything. We shall do as little as possible. We too can make the spaghetti that is sold during the festival, but ... The optimal thing is to let others do everything and only own the brand."

VALUE FROM INTANGIBLES

There is no need for a detailed history of the global economy here, but one should remember that the time when all value was created in tangible, material activities is long gone. Increasingly the global economy puts a premium on all those sorts of hard to define, intangible and often immaterial aspects of life and business.

Thus the value of some of the world's biggest companies today is based less on the sum of their factories, machines, trucks and so on than it is on their ideas, brands and copyrights. What is Coca-Cola if not a brand and a recipe? What is Microsoft if not a brand and a collection of copyrights for computer software? Brands and copyrights are seldom things you can hold in your hand, but nevertheless they can be created, protected and can generate value.

This basically implies four steps:

1. Generate ideas and express them. It is the expression of ideas that creates intellectual property. Ideas themselves cannot be owned, only their expression in a specific way.

2. Keep the intellectual property. This means you should be careful about the content of agreements and avoid selling the copyright, unless perhaps the price is very high.

3. Generate value from intellectual property. Rights can be sold in the same way as tangible assets. Perhaps more importantly, there is an opportunity to make money from various types of licensing rights.

4. Protect the intellectual property. A successful work will sooner or later be copied. Are you protected against this? Registration of trademarks, designs and artistic works

is a good first step to prevent unfair exploitation of your creations. Invest in professional legal help. However, another question is how far are you willing to go in order to stop the copy-cat?

FEEL FREE – BUT STAY PUT

Intellectual property is for most creative businesses the only really valuable asset they have. It forms the basis for the valuation of companies and is the essential ingredient all investors will look at.

The need to protect intellectual property has been subject to wide ranging and fierce series of debates in recent years.

In areas where digital distribution of intellectual property is possible – such as software, film, music, or games – 'piracy' has become something everyone needs to think about when they design strategies to profit from their creativity. However, 'pirates' exist in all industries and can be easily identifiable local imitators or hard to track down pirates from emerging economies. It is important then to think carefully about where your goods or services get exposure and to think carefully about how you will monitor the grey and black markets for your goods.

But hey, did we not just talk earlier about thinking about giving away certain products for free and getting paid from others? Giving away your software and songs for free can indeed be a good idea if this leads to higher prices on other products.

However, it is one thing to give away something you own for free and quite another thing to transfer the underlying rights. The former lets you keep control and the opportunity to change strategies in the future.

Chose to fight or love piracy – whatever the strategy, the point is you should have a strategy for this.

CASE: SWEDEN ROCK
MUSIC.
NORJE, SWEDEN.

The lesson of Sweden Rock's turnaround is one for everybody interested in expanding businesses you didn't think was scalable.

What is Sweden Rock? Some would say it is an annual rock festival in the south of Sweden. This is quite true: it is in fact Sweden's biggest festival and a giant in the heavy metal genre that manages to attract names like Judas Priest, Aerosmith and Motörhead. However, others will think of the music magazine that also bears the name Sweden Rock.

Although a rock festival since 1992, Sweden Rock is now a brand that is used on a number of different products. Sweden Rock is – in addition to a magazine and a festival – also a booking agency, an Internet-based music store, an event organizer in general and a restaurant.

> "The name can be put on all things that have to do with rock," says Michael Ivarsson, the former CEO of Sweden Rock. "The goal is to 'plug in' the name in people's mind."

Ivarsson started the turnaround of the festival's fortunes in 2001 after the previous organization behind it went bankrupt. Before taking over the festival, he had worked with heavy metal and rock for 25 years. He had had his own company and worked with production, distribution as well as retail. He knew the industry, he had contacts and he had experience.

The strategy he put into place was to grow slowly and to begin by getting costs under control. However, right from the start a key focus was to build Sweden's most important brand in the heavy metal genre.

Michael Ivarsson asked an existing rock magazine to change its name and worked a lot with the international industry press, instead of with general Swedish press, in order to achieve credibility in the niche.

A target group was identified and festival bands that would appeal to this group were booked. According to Michael,

> "classical bands that people know and with a high nostalgia factor."

Since the takeover, the number of tickets sold has increased from 7,500 to 35,200. Revenues have increased at an even faster pace: since the tickets cost about four times more than they did and since more activities have been added to the company. Sweden Rock's turnover last year was about 7 million Euros, with a profit of 1.9 million Euros.

"The festival is the foundation," says Michael Ivarsson.

The festival is also what mainly constitutes 'the festival company'. The other activities are in other companies and according to Michael are most of all about boosting the brand. Despite this all the other activities are taken as very serious business propositions. The magazine now comes out nine times a year and is the leader in its niche. The web shop is a good marketplace for the festival artists and Sweden Rock's own material, such as tickets, books and compilations, but also a good way to build relationships with its customer group.

So are the activities there to market the festival or are they businesses in themselves?

> "They must all make money on their own. If not, they either have to be turned around or cut off. There is no idealism in this and it is not an option to take a loss."

When asked if doing all these other activities risks diminishing their focus on the core product, Ivarsson says that he has a very clear focus on the core business but that in reality the core business is built up of several components.

So what is the core business? The festival is the obvious answer. Nonetheless Ivarsson acknowledges that the core business might as well be to build and make money on the intellectual property the festival generates – the brand.

Ivarsson also points out that the organization is streamlined: with only 12–13 people in the main organization, almost all of whom operate through their own companies. For other operations they do not want to have in-house, very thorough agreements are made with subcontractors they trust.

The 'sideline' activities are far from easy add-ons to the core business and each involves very specialized skills: such as the online music store. These are also affiliated with the festival company through so called 'premium agreements'. It is in this sense a rather complex organization, with several companies, but Michael Ivarsson managed them all with regard to strategy, management and budget. A few of these companies also own some parts of the festival company and get returns in terms of dividends.

So what you thought was a festival, or perhaps a conglomerate, was in fact a company licensing its brand to different activities, which it just happens to manage too.

AXIOM 6: I SHOULD DO WHAT IS EXPECTED OF ME IN BUSINESS: MAXIMIZE PROFIT

LESSONS

- DECIDE HOW YOU CAN PROFIT FROM YOUR BUSINESS AND REMEMBER THAT THERE ARE OTHER REWARDS THAN MONEY.

- HAVING OTHER GOALS THAN FINANCIAL ONES DOES NOT IMPLY THAT YOU CAN BE IRRESPONSIBLE IN BUSINESS. WITH GROWTH, NOT LEAST WITH EXTERNAL FINANCING AND EMPLOYEES, COMES RESPONSIBILITY.

- THE ORGANIZATIONAL FORM YOU CHOOSE WILL HELP REFLECT AND ARTICULATE YOUR VISION: SOCIAL ENTREPRENEURSHIP DOES NOT ALWAYS NEED A COMPANY FORMAT.

- EVEN IF YOU HAVE SOME OTHER GOALS THAN MAKING MONEY, FORMULATE A STRATEGY AND PLAN FOR ALL OF THEM. INCLUDE THEM IN THE EVALUATION PROCESS: WHAT GETS MEASURED OFTEN GETS DONE.

IT IS UP TO YOU

MONEY IS NOT EVERYTHING

Not everybody wants to expand their business. Neither is it necessary. It is up to the entrepreneur to decide.

The first question is therefore: what do you want? And act accordingly.

Maybe you want to put some extra money into increasing the quality of what you offer, even though this might not make financial sense?

Maybe you want to make a statement or offer an opinion that no one wants to pay you for?

Rewards come in many forms, not only as money. Therefore, think carefully about what other goals you may have and what achieving them will involve (for you and for your business).

The Icelandic designer Tinna Gunnarsdottir, for instance, keeps her production mostly inhouse and limits herself to a smaller scale. She does this to ensure that she can stay true to the reason she started out with a gallery – to promote Icelandic design. She keeps production in Iceland in order to help further strengthen the Icelandic handcraft industry.

Your company might also be a tool for living the life you want to live – in the right industry, with the right people, in the right area of the city, with the right clients, with travel to the right places, with something you have a passion for and cannot imagine being without.

Small businesses often want to stay small. One reason is to control everything. Another reason is that staying small enables a certain degree of freedom.

LACK OF MONEY CAN BE EVERYTHING

Even if your goals have more to do with doing good than making money having a handle on your financial resources is a necessary step. In the long-term goals that are to be pursued within the framework of a business – whether they are personal goals or about social entrepreneurship – need to be planned for in combination with your organisational planning. Having goals other than financial ones does not imply that you can be, or are, irresponsible with your business.

However noble something might be, it must not jeopardize the organization: what good are an organization's goals if it cannot survive to realize them?

This is especially true if other people are involved in your organization: clients, investors or employees. Certainly, this is the case if you expand your business. With expansion comes responsibility.

A particularly important issue is the need to have the papers in place when reporting to the tax authorities or meeting with the bank or other financers. You never know when you might need a bank loan or another grant.

Keeping good records is also about acting seriously businesswise, which is a must in order to cut good deals. And why shouldn't you? Remember, the better you run the business, the more you can make it work for your goals, whatever they might be.

A good way to balance the different goals is to use an evaluation model that includes different variables, not only the ones involving marketing or profit margins. This also helps to formulate your overall strategy, which is another important part of running a business (read more about this in the next Axiom). Carefully formulating, and constantly reappraising, your goals involves developing some concrete measures of the outcomes (and costs) of the activities each goal involves. Separating each goal from the others is a good way to start; follow this by listing under each goal the activities involved; from this you can develop a cost and time plan for each activity as well as a definite outcome (so that you know when to stop and pat yourself on the back).

Often what gets measured gets done.

CASE: ROCKPARTY
NOT-FOR-PROFIT MEMBERS' ORGANISATION
WORKING WITH MUSIC, CONCERTS AND FESTIVALS.
HULTSFRED, SWEDEN.

The example of Rockparty demonstrates that you can be as serious with money as any business, whilst not actually running a business; and that you can, with the right organisation in place, choose to run projects even if they are not profitable.

Sound stupid? Not if you deal with non-profit organizations. Then you have other goals than just maximizing profits. This is the case with Rockparty, a not-for-profit association that generates an annual turnover of approximately 7 million Euros from some very commercial activities.

The association was established in 1981 in the small town of Hultsfred. Although now involving several activities and many employees, their main focus is the annual rock festival that attracts around 25,000 people to Hultsfred for four days of music each year. Established in 1986, the festival is one of the main events in the Swedish musical calendar. Many successful bands and artists, for instance The Cardigans and Kent, started out on the demo stage, which is reserved for those with no record deal.

Originally, Rockparty was founded to make life better for the youths in this small town and involved organizing parties featuring some of Sweden's most popular artists. In the early years most of the work was done by the four founders on a voluntary basis, but as the organization grew help was needed with the business administration. Initially the only source of revenue was ticket sales and the surplus was invested in growth as well as other activities.

The purpose from the beginning – to create a better place to live in – is still one of the main goals for Rockparty. These goals are written into the association's constitution, which also ensures that decisions are as democratic as possible by allotting all members one vote. Co-founder Putte Svensson:

> "We are working in the spirit of the organisation's charter, which is about developing music-related events and activities for the use of young people in the region. But we have also been involved with young people's situation in many ways. For instance, we noted that education was missing – so we started one, and after that a few more. We have been a kind of modern social entrepreneur with our roots in music and culture."

What you give is also what you get back – and Rockparty has had great help from the community. Hundreds of volunteers work each year with the festival – a few of them wanting to take part in something they feel provides something good, others are there to help their own organizations as 5 percent of ticket revenue goes to other associations that help out.

Although successful, Rockparty has had its hard times and sometimes needed support. The first time was in 1987 when only one bank agreed to lend money, but no more than a fraction of the total debt which amounted to 20,000 Euros. However, with ten friends who personally guaranteed their share, the debt could be paid back.

Even if Rockparty has a high profile and has even been acknowledged by the government for its achievements, it has still problems being taken seriously by financiers.

The first suspicion is about the activity: 'music, how can that generate money?' The second is about the type of organization.

Financers' problems with the organisational form forced Rockparty to form a private company when the concert hall Metropol was to be built. The bank wanted a regular company as a borrower. A company was their natural counterpart, whereas a not-for-profit association regulated by the members – irrespective of previous successes – felt risky. Putte Svensson:

> "I would say there is a prejudice that non-profit associations are not as good as regular companies at doing busi-

ness; just because it is not their primary goal to make a profit.

Of course, the driving force among many of the employees is about something other than making money. But it does not need to imply a contradiction. It's a question of management to control this."

Indeed this is equally true of private organizations: where the employees have – and need – other personal incentives than just the idea that they are benefiting shareholders.

Another issue for private financers is that an association is quite easily dissolved or can change its regulations and goals quickly. Nevertheless, a company can also change direction and rapidly dissolving companies are far from rare. A key problem though is responsibility since the board members of not-for-profit organizations are personally responsible for the finances whereas owners of limited companies are not personally responsible in the case of bankruptcy.

As their activities have grown to become major events with major costs and risks, the board of Rockparty has contemplated reorganizing into a company structure in order to facilitate the contacts with banks, other investors and the tax authorities. Putte suggests that such a move would affect the 'soul' of what they founded.

He also adds that the current model implies benefits when it comes to financing: major sums are needed for the advances big artists now demand. There can be occasions when 300,000 Euros are needed instantly, but only for three weeks. However, for Rockparty a trusted network sometimes helps them avoid the banking system.

"We don't deal much with banks anymore," says Putte Svensson, "That process takes too much time. Borrowing privately is so much easier. We now have long-term relations with individuals but also with customers and suppliers who lend money."

These loans are mostly ranging from 50,000 to 100,000 Euros and are mostly informal.

"Papers are written, but in practise that is only a formality for the bookkeeping. The handshake is what matters."

CASE: TINNA GUNNARS- DOTTIR
INDUSTRIAL DESIGN.
REYKJAVIK, ICELAND.

To run a creative company is not always a question about growth – in many cases it is more about personal expression. Tinna Gunnarsdottir is an Icelandic industrial designer, who in 2005 received the Designer of the Year award by the Icelandic Design Forum and the City of Reykjavik. She graduated with a degree in three dimensional design from a design school in London in 1992 and after her graduation ran a gallery and workshop in Reykjavik with the goal of producing her own designs herself.

> "Of course I had to do all kinds of other jobs as well, as there was no financing available, at least not to my knowledge, and then I learned that you can often do a lot for very little money."

Although the gallery was successful, even attracting the attention of MTV at one point, it took a lot of her time and there was less time to work on her own designs. So after three years of running the gallery she moved to Milan to do a Master's degree in industrial design. Through this international school she built a network, which has been important to opening her eyes to the possibilities of international production, as well as helping her better understand the importance of international exhibitions.

Tinna has quite an impressive exhibition record, and has been invited to participate in important international exhibitions, yet she finds it hard to take the next step to international production and does not even know if she wants to. There are two sides to this.

First, she does not want her life and work to be taken over by one product, and second, she says:

> "I am personally not interested in persuading people of the brilliance of my own products; while I was running the gallery I even found it difficult to accept money from people. I like it best if I can work in peace and quiet far away from anyone.
>
> Of course I know the argument, that you can learn a lot from being in contact with the clients but I don't want to service the client too much. I would rather want to be surprised by the buyers, like with my bug mats. At first I thought I would never sell them, but I do."

While Tinna was undecided about pursuing international production she found out that many of her fellow designers were starting out with their own small scale production. Keeping the scale small has become important to her: she can do it herself in Iceland; she can manage her own time; and she feels the work is authentic.

To finance the production Tinna has sought grants, rather than direct investment. Although she is educated as an industrial designer, she has found that she falls between two types of grants; the industry grants aimed at facilitating prototype production and traditional artists' funds.

The question still remains whether she should bring some of her designs to the big design companies who have international distribution and marketing networks, but Tinna doesn't really know what would be the best way to do so.

> "Should I try to sell it to them directly, or should I go through someone?"

But one thing is clear, if Tinna is going into production on a larger scale than she is doing now, she would need a business person with her:

> "it is just too much to do all on your own."

What is important here is that Tinna is constantly thinking about what she wants from what she does and is not just chasing money and work for the sake of it.

AXIOM 7:
PLANS ALWAYS TURN OUT TO BE WRONG, AND SINCE I AM SO BUSY I DON'T BOTHER WITH THEM

LESSONS

- IT IS NOT THE PLAN THAT IS IMPORTANT, BUT THE ASSUMPTIONS, THE GOALS AND THE STRATEGY.

- WORK ON YOUR BUSINESS, NOT ONLY IN YOUR BUSINESS.

- HAVE THE PAPER IN PLACE. ACT AS IF YOU WOULD SELL THE COMPANY TOMORROW.

- YOUR BUSINESS SHOULD NOT BE TOO DEPENDENT ON YOU, AT LEAST NOT ALWAYS.

- CREATE A SYSTEM THAT WORKS FOR YOU, WHICH MEANS ORGANIZING YOUR PROCESSES AND LOGISTICS.

- ACTIVELY SEEK AND ACT ON ADVICE.

CREATING A SYSTEM

WORK ON YOUR BUSINESS

One of the most common reasons why many small businesses fail, go bankrupt or simply don't reach their potential is the lack of system. This is also the biggest concern for customers, suppliers, banks and investors when they contemplate a relationship with a small business.

This is perhaps especially true for enterprises that are based around one or a few key people. The chance is that something unexpected or unwanted will eventually happen to people in micro-businesses. Indeed, doing everything yourself is probably empowering but also a great way to burn out. So what will happen if the driving person or talent gets sick or just gets tired of business?

A business plan is a good start in order to manage and plan for some of these eventualities and to create a system that will work for you. Business planning is not just about having paper to convince banks with – it is about working on your business, not only in your business.

Such planning means setting up a system that helps you get a grip on the whole operation – from the fun stuff to the boring stuff. A system helps you avoid spending all your time chasing things, re-learning things, finding things and playing catch up. A good system captures all the elements of different activities: not just the costs and goals but the processes and paper involved which each activity. For example, systems for organising supplies, sub-contractors, production and logistics also mean systems of contracts and agreements so that suppliers, customers, etc. can be managed and evaluated.

Much of the above can sound rather dull to people interested in pursuing a dream and there is a tendency to concentrate all the efforts on the creative side of the business.

Many small businesses think that they have to produce everything, but production is rarely the difficult part. The processes and paper behind your production or insourcing, such as managing the supply chain, however, often need time and can be costly if left to chance. Consider Wal-Mart, one of the biggest companies in the world. They do not in-house any production but have very advanced and well-thought out processes for getting it done, in and on time.

The fashion company Odd Molly is another good example of a business that has emphasized the business model (see the next Case). The company relies on a system that not only involves production and distribution, but also a strong emphasis on liquidity planning and branding.

A business plan clearly lays out your product, your needs, your potential markets and margins, and your realistic expectations and growth strategy. A good plan should help you understand the business processes underpinning your firm and help you understand what you are getting into. It will also be useful when approaching people – such as bank managers – who might know nothing about your field.

Articulate what has to be articulated. A one-page summary is often good as a start. (This is not about writing a novel.)

The main thing is that the business plan lets you think about goals and assumptions: where do you want to go and what does it take to get there?

GET SERIOUS AND SEEK ADVICE

Does this sound difficult?

If so, it is not a reason for ignoring it. Too often plans for the business's development and its financing tend to be sidelined, skimmed over or, at worst, ignored and seen as a distraction. You might remember Jesper Brodersen admitting that: "I hate money, and I am scared of money, it really blocks me."

If you get blocked, get a plumber. Make sure you have someone who can get to grips with the messy stuff you don't want your hands in – someone who can act for you but also translate your needs to other people. Investors, for instance, often use a very different vocabulary to evaluate projects and ideas; quite different from how an artistic or cultural idea is evaluated. Whilst buying a Linguaphone can help you learn the language, often hiring a native guide is a quicker way to get through the jungle.

To actively seek and act on advice has proved to be vital to many of the entrepreneurs we have talked to. Advice, however, often comes at a price: which can be a good thing. If you pay for a service then people's take on the task will often be more professional. A board that gets paid will know that you are serious about your business.

Similarly, if the price involves giving away or discounting shares of your company – chances are that you will have committed investors who will share your objectives of turning your business into a successful one. Several successful small businesses say that having investors involved not just money but useful advice. (However, getting the right investors for your business is critical.)

HAVING THE PAPER IN PLACE

You might have a business plan with a great system outlined and a dedicated board – but plans seldom work out in a perfect way.

You cannot control everything, which raises another point: planning is a constant process. This, however, requires that you have the paper in place:

– Having the paper in place will enable you to make quick decisions and adjustments, since you know the current status of your company.

– Having the paper in place will enable you to get the correct advice when you ask for it, since the actual preconditions will be known.

Moreover, one important reason why the fashion company Odd Molly was able to get investment and go public so fast was the emphasis on keeping good records. They acted as if they were a publicly listed company several years before actually going public. If you think you might like to be bigger in the future then act like a grown up from day one.

It is also a question of being taken seriously and controlling your time. Making time for routine activities such as keeping records and having the paper in place will mean that you can come up with information as needed – because at some point you might be asked for them and really need them: If not by investors then by the tax man.

CASE: ODD MOLLY
FASHION.
STOCKHOLM, SWEDEN.

If the fashion company Odd Molly would have a soundtrack it might be "You'll never walk alone."

The story of this Swedish company – which five years after it was founded sold clothes for 13 million Euros in more than 30 countries and was listed on the OMX Nordic Exchange – is a story about what a good system, a division of labour and a blend of different experiences can do.

It started out with three people with different roles, but sharing the same idea – that fashion is for everybody.

There was the branding person, Per Holknekt, who had previously built several companies thanks to an emphasis on their brands.

There was the designer, Karin Jimfelt-Ghatan, who had a clear idea about the actual clothes.

There was also the organizer, Christer Andersson, who invested SEK 500 thousand and was in charge of administration and the organization during the first years. Since the founders worked without a salary in the first year, this initial investment was enough to get going and make the first collection; though not enough for an office space.

The company is still built on these three elements: brand, design and organization.

The co-founder Christer Andersson points to the business model as a critical factor in their success (in addition to the fact that the customers actually like the Odd Molly brand and clothes):

> "We only produce if an order is placed. This implies a minimum of credit risk, no stock and that revenues and results can be calculated six months in advance."

The system is constructed so that money goes out at the same time money comes in. This model also enables expansion with a minimum of capital. Their invoices are sold to a factoring company (finance companies that purchase invoices at a discount and then collect them themselves) in order to get cash faster. At the other end of the business they negotiate with their suppliers a credit period which lasts until the clothes are actually delivered – matching the credit period that Odd Molly's customers receive. In this way they can minimise the time between paying suppliers and getting paid: essentially they maximise their turnover whilst minimizing the cash they need.

During its second year – 2003 – Odd Molly acquired a 1.5 million SEK investment: one third from a bank; one third from the state-owned investor Almi; and one third from a private investor. Not much for an expanding fashion company but perhaps just enough:

> "I think it was fortunate that we did not have so much money. We have been profitable every year except the first year and we were able to keep the majority of the company," says co-founder Christer Andersson.

The current CEO, Christina Tillman, took office in 2005. She started working to attract more capital and another 2 million SEK was acquired in 2005 from seven private investors. She wrote the investment memorandum herself, but she was hardly a freshman having worked, among other things, as COO at the multinational cosmetics company Face Stockholm.

Two years later Odd Molly went public at First North: an alternative stock market for growth companies. The share price soared directly after the stock was introduced and the company has been under a lot of media and investor attention since then.

> "Actually, no big changes have been necessary," says Christina Tillman. "We have had the strategy to act as if we were publicly listed for a long time."

All the papers have been in place from the beginning. The emphasis on quality in everything is clear. This means that Odd Molly has required high standards from all involved: suppliers, distributors, and themselves.

> "We want to deliver correctly and on time, and make sure that our suppliers get paid as agreed."

The system also involves the brand strategy. The company depicts itself as "a brand with a mind, a heart and a conscience." The clothes themselves are meant to be easily identifiable thanks to external labels with a unique type-face and a special rinsing fluid. New collections come with a theme, presented with by-lines such as "vive la difference," "you are perfect because you are not" and "living tenfold." These themes are backed by a PR strategy, and retailers are given materials that introduce them to the new theme.

Indeed, the company is conscious that everywhere it appears should be in line with its brand and values. At the company's website you are welcomed with the headline: "Hello, we are Odd Molly, we hope you are well." Then, you will find messages such as "Odd Molly uncorporated," "celebrating yourselves" and "pleasure business." At the door to the office in the Old Town in Stockholm, the sign is of the type you see outside private apartments and says: "ODD MOLLY LIVES HERE."

Although every company has its key people – this goes for Odd Molly too – the brand and the business model imply that "Molly" is hardly a one-person show. Odd Molly does not walk (or write business plans) alone.

CASE: COPENHAGEN BOMBAY
FILM PRODUCTION.
COPENHAGEN, DENMARK.

Business, like most of life, is made up of a myriad of routines. These routines, although easy to forget when thinking up grand business plans, are at the very core of any cost estimation. When Sarita Christensen and Anders Morgenthaler decided to break out of Zentropa where they were both working, Sarita admitted that she knew nothing about business plans, but she did know about budgeting, and routines and took it from there.

> "I had never seen a business plan in my life and I didn't look at one before I made my own, which was four pages in Excel. But this was the way I could understand it, this is my language. And potential investors and banks where very positive, the costs where very well defined, very specific, into all kinds of details and the upside was not very optimistic, it was quite in the long run."

The spreadsheet was indeed very specific, down to headphones for the animation studio and the cost of having a student assistant working at the company. With this four-page detailed spreadsheet Sarita was able to finance her and Anders Morgenthaler's new production company for four years, only a few months after they left their jobs at Zentropa. Upon leaving the big film production company they had just finished working on the project Princess, which Anders created and directed and Sarita produced. Both of them had ambitions to make original children's and youth content; something which was not a high priority at Zentropa.

The decision to start a new company took only a week to make, when Sarita was offered a promotion within Zentropa she knew she would either have to leave her ambition to make content for youth and children or leave the company. She chose the latter. Anders and Sarita did not leave Zentropa with ill feelings, in fact Peter Aalbæk (co-owner of Zentropa) was the first person they looked to for financing. His response was, that no matter how much he believed in the company, he could not support the spin-off without risking other employees getting similar ideas, and naturally he could not risk Zentropa losing everyone. This left Sarita looking to other film production companies, the biggest one in Denmark being Nordisk Film.

The timing of the spin-off could not have been better. Anders and Sarita were in Cannes, promoting Princess, which was the only Danish film in Cannes and received quite some interest. This meant they did not have to go door-to-door with their business plan as everyone knew about their plans. The initial finances where negotiated with Nordisk Film in only a month but during this time Sarita had to revise the budget a few times.

> "I just had to sit down and write everything over and I had to redo the business plan, I wouldn't say several times but in my negotiations with Nordisk film I had to redo the business plan maybe three times but that's how it is, that's part of the negotiation. I have to redo it for myself and find out what I can live with. What is reasonable and what is not realistic anymore and what is someone else's ambition."

Nordisk Film agreed to fund one third of the company, which gave them one third of the shares and a seat on the three person board. But more financing was needed. This was partly gained through a business angel, Vibeke Winderløv, who bought 5% of the company but brought with her an extensive network as well as experience in making business plans and managing firms. The last part of the company was financed through a bank loan.

But financing the company was not the only project Sarita had to solve in the initial months.

"Besides doing the business plan I had job interviews, I had lawyers to talk to, and I had to find a place for the company and talk to phone companies and internet set-ups and everything, and I had to do everything myself."

The detailed plan Sarita made worked in the negotiations with investors and banks because of the careful detail to everyday routines and costs. In planning their projects they are careful to use a mix of people but to remain close to the core activity.

"So I have to be very close to the production, so I can see what the potential is, how much we can optimize. You can always optimize and sometimes you have to reorganize. That is a very interesting thing, it is kind of research in itself every day to see what is the potential of your company."

One of the ways CHP Bombay does optimize is to rent out some of its office space to freelancers who then also work on some projects with them. They are also very aware of using different kinds of platforms for their production, as well as a mixture of genres. But in spite of success in financing the company and getting it up and running, Sarita does not intend or wish for the company to grow beyond its current size. Her argument is that growth would cost them their focus.

AXIOM 8:
MY PRODUCT IS GREAT, IT'S UNIQUE, IT WILL FIND ITS CUSTOMERS

LESSONS

- SELLING THE PRODUCTS IS WHAT MAKES A BUSINESS SURVIVE AND THRIVE. TOO OFTEN INFERIOR PRODUCTS WIN IN THE MARKET-PLACE DUE TO A BETTER FOCUS ON MARKETING AND GETTING TO CUSTOMERS.

- YOUR COMPANY AND YOUR PRODUCTS EXIST IN A VERY CROWDED MARKETPLACE. THINK CAREFULLY ABOUT YOUR COMPETITIVE ADVANTAGE, FOR INSTANCE WITH REGARD TO PRICE, DIFFERENTIATION AND BRANDING.

- PLANNING FOR MARKETING AND SALES INCLUDES SPOTTING A GAP IN THE MARKET. WHAT CAN YOU DO THAT COMPETITORS CAN'T? WHAT CAN YOU DO THAT NO ONE ELSE HAS DONE?

- DON'T FORGET THAT THE WORLD IS OUT THERE. SMALL NATIONS MIGHT NOT BE POPULATED BY LARGE NUMBERS OF CUSTOMERS - MAYBE YOUR BUSINESS MODEL NEEDS TO CROSS BORDERS.

GET IT OUT THERE

SALES

The world is not fair. Remember videotapes? It is not always the superior product that survives in the market. Betamax might have been technically better than VHS but that was not enough. A strong product is important, but not worth anything if you cannot reach the customers and persuade them that they want your services.

This does not only mean that people will know about and like the product (branding), but also that it is easily available (distribution) and at a price they are willing to pay (pricing and sales). Hopefully, the customers will be so satisfied with you or the product that they will come back to you.

Not focusing enough on sales is one of the most common mistakes small, and especially creative, enterprises make. Because you can never count on – no matter how fantastic your product is – that the customer will find you. It is unfortunately you who have to ask for the first dance.

You also have to analyze your competitors. This is crucial in order to position yourself with regard to price and potential customers. What customers are best suited for your product (target group)? How can you make a difference in relation to competitors (competitive advantage)?

Branding is thus only one part of a wider strategy called differentiation. Focusing on how you can persuade consumers that you are different and that there is no real substitute for your product is the key factor behind most businesses. It is also something that your competitors are also very good at and thus something you need to plan for from day one. So a fashion designer might want to start thinking first about what 'story' they want to tell before focusing on the clothes, belts and shoes that might communicate it.

FINDING YOUR ROLE

Selling products often involves a great deal of planning (see the previous section about creating a system). Selling fashion clothes: should you use a distributor or sell directly to shops? Should you start your own shop? If you are producing music: should you aim for the American market from the beginning or start with your local market?

Making a choice does not imply you are stuck with it forever. Rather, see the next step as one move closer to a bigger goal. Murlyn Music did not start out with the goal to work with Madonna. Instead, the CEO, Christian Wåhlberg, emphasized the importance of breaking down the bigger plan into smaller actions.

A planning process also needs to be constantly revised. It is therefore important to be aware of what is happening in the market and in the world – since both are changing all the time.

The collapse of the record industry is one such global change that can provide both chaos and possibilities for those wanting to be involved in music. Mr. Destiny, who organizes the Iceland Airwaves Music Festival, says that suddenly he has to pay for artists in a way that never happened before when the artists made money on selling records. Another example is how Murlyn Music has reorganized the company due to the structural changes in the market, which implied that the record labels – their customers – have much less purchasing power. Conversely, the changing ways in which consumers find and consume music has opened up possibilities and profits for new types of participants: from Apple to non-label MySpace bands.

In any case, dedicating resources for sales, as well as for marketing in general, is critical. Putting everything into the production process may be fun but will not help you much in the end – if you cannot afford to continue.

However, maybe you want to devote all your time and energy to production. A good solution then is to find another person who works with sales.

Don't want to employ a salesperson or take in a partner? There are companies, agents and licensees that you can outsource to or who will work on commission. If you are trading far from home these people can also be locally knowledgeable and connected in ways you will never be.

FINDING THE WHOLE

You also have to realize that it is not the customers' fault if your product does not sell. Rather, you have to listen to the customers' wants before someone else does.

Finding a gap or a niche in the market is a key factor for success.

- The fashion company Nikita spotted that there were no clothes for women skaters and snowboarders.
- The marketing bureau Clutch started in the field of digital marketing when the Internet was relatively new but knew that there would soon be a need for their services.
- Bonnier Tidskrifter (Bonnier Magazines Sweden) prepares thoroughly before every release with extensive market research, both analyzing reader and advertiser groups.

Remember too that there is a whole world out there, and distribution has become so much easier in general. Perhaps you cannot take advantage of the opportunities of digital distribution, but in comparison to a divided east-and-west-type-of-world more markets are now open and in many places people have money to spend.

Equally, with cheaper shipping and digital distribution it is easier than ever to think not about one or two or three markets but instead about niches and subcultures and strange interests that are not really big in any one place: but globally form a large customer base.

CASE: BONNIER TIDSKRIFTER
MAGAZINE PUBLISHING.
STOCKHOLM, SWEDEN.

In many creative industries there is hardly a scarcity of new ideas and innovative thinking. In large media and publishing firms it might be hard to keep control of what is happening and thus end up with products that are internal babies that few in the real world want to buy. All sorts of factors add to this picture:

- The mantra found in many publishing firms that "we must risk to fail" – encourages innovation but also risk taking.

- That all directors are ultimately there to expand their respective business units.

- That in big organisations there are often hundreds of people with big egos, who know best and whose dream it is to show-it-off to the world.

Needless to say, there is hardly any scarcity of new ideas. The art is to manage them.

This is what Ulrika Saxon does. She is the CEO of Bonnier Tidskrifter – a giant in the Nordic magazine industry with 154 million Euros in revenues, publishing about 600 issues yearly, employing 500 people and working with thousands of freelancers. The company's oldest title was launched in 1892.

"What we have been good at is to know when to cut off projects," says Ulrika Saxon. "Although many projects are initiated and managed by an enthusiast who came up with the idea, there must be no drama about trying and failing."

The costs are easy to assess in advance, so what decides a stoplight or a green-light for a project is an idea of the project's potential. The bigger the potential, the longer their patience. Ulrika Saxon explains:

> "For a niche title with an estimated circulation of 25,000 copies, there is no starting run. It has to survive on its own merits from day one. But for a title that might sell 100,000 copies, it can require three years before break-even."

How do they choose among all ideas?

> "The editorial idea has to be unique ... and there has to be a clear and measurable gap in the market. As market leaders we put a great effort in the ambition to be the best publishers. This is important to be able to attract and keep the best; the best employees, readers and advertisers."

New ideas go through an internal process where they are showcased.

> "What happens is that the editorial idea is visualized with examples of covers. However, there is often too much focus on this in the presentation and too little on the market research. Is there a gap out there? How big is it? What does that mean in terms of profit? Are there any international benchmarks? The best presentations balance these sides of a new project."

When starting new titles, the preparations are thorough and worked through by a special team, three or four people during the development phase, including the person behind the idea. Ulrika Saxon describes how people are chosen for a new project:

> "Experience is important. Dedication is unbeatable."

The risk, however, is that enthusiasts lose sight of the market and become too optimistic or overestimate likely sales. Therefore, there are always three functions in any new or existent project:

The Marketing Director who can understand and quantify the gap in the market, probably with the help of market research such as focus groups. This person also looks at distribution, public relations and release.

The Editor-in-Chief, often a source of ideas and a bit like an artist, is responsible for the brand of the title and therefore higher in the ranks than the Marketing Director. Still, it is the Marketing Director's role to help balance creative with marketing ambitions. The personal chemistry between these two is of great importance.

The Controller, who is not operative in the project but works directly with the business area manager. There are four such areas and seven controllers at Bonnier Tidskrifter. The controller's role is act like an external auditor and to slow down or even cut-off projects if necessary.

Ulrika Saxon previously headed a sub-unit of Bonnier Tidskrifter, Bonzoo, with the aim to be more flexible and innovative. This division was founded eight years ago in a situation when the market of new niche-ideas started to boom on the magazine market. It is now integrated into the parent company.

> "I learnt to prioritize time for preparations, to dare to brake before you say go. You only have one chance to give a first impression."

CASE: CLUTCH MEDIA
NEW MEDIA.
HAMAR, NORWAY.

Claus Morten Pedersen had been working in the media since university and wanted to start his own business in what interested him the most: digital marketing over the Internet. His business – Clutch Media – is a small new media firm that produces film for the Internet, TV, and movie theatres. In addition, they offer design, photo, print and DVD services as well as web solution. They are involved in a wide range of activities but their main business focus is on different forms of Internet marketing and adverts something that even now is still in its infancy.

Claus Morten was not just interested in starting a business in a new area but also in moving to a new area. He contacted science parks in his old home town of Hamar which offered him space in a newly started business incubator. The rent was low and they also helped him out with administrative and practical tasks plus some business advice.

At first he was dubious about establishing his own firm, he had a good job at one of the biggest media firms in Norway. He was not sure about the size and the competence of the market (especially in Hamar where he wanted to move), and was not convinced that the customers knew what they wanted, or if they would dare do something new. Things have turned out well and he now has a growing company. Even though there are advantages to being in a bigger city like Oslo where there are many and more knowledgeable customers, there are many advantages to being where he is: things are not so hectic and the competition is not so cut throat.

His start-up financing came from the public organisation Innovation Norway (Innovasjon Norge) which has "products and services intended to help boost innovation in business and industry nationwide, foster regional development and promote

IN." The money from IN helped him to "hit the ground running."

The financing process with IN went reasonably easy. In 2001, when he started his business, Internet marketing was only just beginning but he managed to find people who understood that there was potential in this niche (and that the niche might eventually become mainstream). They understood that he had identified a niche – services to fuel Internet marketing – and that there was real commercial potential in this.

Support from IN came with a major condition: compulsory business advice. That is meant to help young businesses through their first difficult years, and includes help with developing business plans and focus. The stress they put on a focused business plan did not fit since it was too early to specialise in developing the Internet marketing niche. This was difficult to get the business consultants to understand since they did not fully understand Clutch's type of business. Claus Morten advised them to use mentors instead: people who had hands-on experience from similar types of businesses but were not in direct competition. This is now more common.

The company has had steady but relatively slow growth. They have never had a bank loan, but he says "If you want to grow, capital is a necessity." They have no debt today. Clutch did not become a limited liability company until 2005.

They have had a mixed experience with banks. They are a growing company but the banks still do not really treat them seriously. For example, when they wanted a line of credit for daily operations, they were required to guarantee it personally and not through the company. He claims that the local banks do not have experience with new business areas. Banks in the countryside understand the needs of agriculture better than those of newer industries. Even if companies present business plans and even potentially dedicated customers, banks are reluctant to give loans.

At the time he started there was a technological revolution. The prices on cameras, editing equipment and such became a lot cheaper. This meant that barriers to entry were lowered and now there are a lot of new companies/competitors. In addition, there are a lot of freelancers. He thinks this is changing now as there is a tendency for businesses to merge and for bigger companies to buy smaller ones. One of the reasons behind this is that speed is getting more important. In big companies it is possible react more quickly.

The Internet marketing business is growing. Both the buyers of advertising and the readers of Internet media are changing and learning. The case of Clutch Media shows how difficult it can be, working with techniques and channels that are rapidly developing: investors find it hard to understand the potential; customers might see the potential but not know what they want. Nonetheless, it shows that successful businesses are often founded on identifying a gap, a niche, or a potential in the marketplace that you believe will grow. It is often about having a belief in your potential customers and about having a passion for what you want to do:

> "We have been doing our hobby, but have succeeded more than we hoped for. It is a cliché, but I think we are successful because we have fun … The most successful periods have been when we have focused on what we think is fun."

CASE: NIKITA
FASHION DESIGN.
REYKJAVIK, HAMBURG,
SAN FRANCISCO, HOSSEGOR.

FINDING A GAP IN THE MARKET IS A KEY FACTOR TO SUCCESS

Nikita started out as a small boardsports/streetwear shop in Iceland. Co-founder and head designer, Heida Birgisdottir, had been involved in fashion design on the side, but as they realized that there was a lack of clothing for girls who skate, the couple behind the shop decided to found a company around designing and producing clothes to fill this category. After nine years in operation Nikita now sells its design products in 1,500 stores in 32 countries with an annual turnover of more than 5 million Euros. According to Runar Omarsson, Nikita took a different road in getting investors to start their business than most other design companies:

> "So many designers think they should get some kind of special treatment when financing their ideas and products – we don't think we are any different than other businesses just because we are selling design products, we have to sell our concept and find capital the same way as everyone else."

The constant dilemma of artists losing their credibility and becoming a 'sell out' if they go into business is a fair enough debate, according to Runar. If an artist or a designer thinks he or she loses credibility by making their creations into business, he or she can keep it as a hobby and work for a living somewhere else. Or the artist can spend his or her life waiting for public (or private) grants, which are usually such small amounts that they don't help in any way. The public grants are rather a kind of recognition for your work but greatly misunderstood by both the provider and the receiver as being a great gate opener to international fame and fortune. According to Runar, the first thing to do is to make the decision whether you want to take the big step and go into business, or keep your creations as a hobby. The main reason why investors or banks don't take designers seriously is because the designers don't do so themselves.

If you decide that you want to go into business, you need to realize your limitations – it is not necessarily expected that you know how to run a business, make business plans, marketing plans, budgets and so forth. But you need to compensate for your limitations by finding the information and sources needed. The founders of Nikita were three – a designer, a marketing person and a finance person – and they complemented each other with their respective areas of expertise. Their idea was to start a business around the concept of clothing "for girls who ride." Together they spent a few days making the business plan which they took to prospective investors.

> "To be taken seriously by prospective investors or banks the designer needs to take him- or herself seriously, meaning that you have to make the decision to go into business. If you decide to go into business you need to be able to answer questions asked by financial people. Questions like who is going to buy your product? Where are you going to sell it? What kind of distribution channels are you going to use? Are you going to sell it directly to stores? Do the retailers have 30 or 60 or 90 days' credit? Do you need more loans? What kind of return on investment is realistic to expect? And what are the exit possibilities?"

Investors and banks said no to Nikita's capital request, and stated it was a hopeless case. The explanation for the refusals was twofold, according to Runar: firstly, because of a lack of a track record of successful investments in the fashion design industry. The investors and the Icelandic state had been badly burned by a few investment flops in the fashion industry and were, understandably, cautious about making the same mistakes again.

And secondly, because Nikita themselves were not well enough prepared. They were not able to explain clearly enough what their concept and competitive advantage was. But Nikita didn't give up the hope for professional investors and when they found a clause on one of the investors' webpage saying that prospective customers could not be refused without an explanation, they contacted them again and asked for another meeting. For that meeting they prepared better, taking the main points of the business plan, presenting them as a slide show and using some more effective techniques to sell their idea.

This retrial was successful and the investor bought 40% of the company. Why the investor didn't refuse for the second time, Runar said:

> "was because they saw that the Nikita group was serious about what they were doing, knew their business and were obviously enthusiastic designers and business people."

It was also crucial that they had at that point in time already received product orders from Japan and Norway, which added some weight to their request.

The investor required a seat on the board, but did not make any claims regarding how to run the business. That was a prerequisite Nikita had, which the investor accepted. But understandably, as Runar stated, the investor wanted a seat on the board to be able to follow the business and give financial advice.

Nikita used the money from the investor mainly in marketing their design and to further develop their product line. The pre-development phase was financed with their own savings and every penny they earned from their store to develop the Nikita product line.

Nikita has had a fast growth rate since launched and has now started to share the knowledge and success with young and upcoming designers within the industry by spending some of their time counselling and helping new businesses in preparing business plans and getting contacts. Nikita offers internships for fashion designers, graphic designers and marketing students, something for which there has not been a tradition in Iceland. In the world at large, however, internships are considered among the main elements in sustaining and developing the industry itself. As the industry has been developing in Iceland, with more successful companies hence less scepticism from the investors' side, it should not be long before the appearance of specialized design investors to support the industry even further. Nikita was started by identifying a gap in the market: a market was not close to home. Investing in growth has meant money but also commitment to investing in people around them.

AXIOM 9:
NEVER SAY NO

LESSONS

- LEARN TO SAY NO AND PLAN WHEN TO EXIT AND WHEN TO STOP AND TAKE STOCK.

- DON'T BE VAIN. BIG IS NOT ALWAYS BEAUTIFUL, ESPECIALLY NOT IN THE LONG RUN.

- GROSS MARGIN, NOT TURNOVER, IS WHAT MAKES A BUSINESS GOOD.

- PROFIT NEXT YEAR WILL NOT HELP YOU TODAY. KEEPING AN EYE ON YOUR CASH FLOW IS NECESSARY. WITH CASH, YOU ARE IN A MUCH BETTER SITUATION TO MAKE AND EXECUTE EFFECTIVE DECISIONS AS WELL AS PLAN FOR THE FUTURE.

- DON'T RUN TOO FAR BEFORE THINKING ABOUT WHERE YOU ARE HEADING OR YOU RISK HITTING A DEAD END.

- PREPARE FOR CYCLES.

MANAGING MONEY

VANITY FAIR

So we have learnt that selling is the most important thing in business.

Applying what you have found out about selling, you love to see new money coming into the company. If the amount in your bank account increases, it has to be good, doesn't it?

Well, not always. Big is not always beautiful. There are risks with this too. A common startup problem is that entrepreneurs chase turnover and new customers so much that they forget about other important aspects of business.

In order to get more orders you introduce special pricing and increase discounts across the board. You start selling to customers you normally wouldn't.

Yes, you need turnover. But turnover should always be judged in relation to your long term gross margins: the difference between revenues and costs. At early stages you may lose money and discount heavily to establish yourself but remember, this is not sustainable in the long term. Also remember that lower prices in some cases can actually make people think less of your services: part of the reason why people like diamonds is because they are really expensive.

When thinking about your turnover and pricing, ask yourself some key questions:

– Do you sell at the right price?

– For how long can you sustain discounts?

– Are you selling too many units? Do you have time?

– What do you signal with your price?

– What do the people who use your services or stock your product signal to other customers?

Sales generate revenue but also costs. If early on you say yes all the time you might find your costs spiralling: you employ new people, you rent a bigger office space, and you buy expensive plane tickets because you don't have time for an hour's wait at the terminal.

All this is great if the revenues exceed the costs or if these costs are part of the bigger plan. If you predict that growth is needed and profitable in the long run. If so, go ahead, even if you have to take a loss during a year or so.

Ulrika Saxon, the CEO of publisher Bonnier Tidskrifter, points out the need to be in control. She says what she learnt is that there is seldom a lack of ideas, but there is a need to prepare thoroughly for exit and for cutting-off early if necessary. You don't sell for the sake of it. You sell because you think it is a good idea in the long run.

Saying no can therefore be the best thing you can do.

RUNNING IN CYCLES

The second issue you should be aware of is that while busy selling, you may forget about one of the most important things in business in addition to sales, namely investment.

You are so busy with the current sales of the current products that you don't have time either for marketing or for planning new products.

Not all products follow the traditional product life cycle – a period of growth followed by a period of maturity followed by an inevitable decline. There are products that seem to be eternally in demand. However, for every Rembrandt there are many, many more products that come and go and follow a cycle of growth-maturity-decline.

- Fashion companies have their natural cycles in terms of seasons and seasonal transitions: spring/summer and autumn/winter. This cycle of change may indeed be intensifying as more and more fashion firms increase the number of seasons so that new products can enter the assortment almost continuously.

- Music companies know that no record or hit lasts forever and that the cycle of establishing yourself is often as hard with the second album as it is with the first.

Even if your industry does not have these types of obvious seasons or cycles, it might be a good idea to think about your business in these terms anyway. If you have a small business you probably don't have a research and development (R&D) department, but make sure you dedicate time for this kind of activity yourself. Likewise, replace the marketing department with allotting/scheduling yourself time for marketing activities.

CASH REALLY IS KING

We said forget about turnover. Now we will say forget about profit.

The cash flow really is what matters most in the short run. If you don't have cash you will immediately land in a situation where you basically have three choices: go bankrupt, borrow money or sell equity.

Borrowing money and selling equity can be good things, but are seldom so when you are in a hurry.

Increasing sales will of course help you to have money in hand, but so will also saving cash you already have. It is therefore important to minimize costs of all sorts, but primarily fixed running costs you cannot recover. You can sell your chair if you must, but you will never get the office rent back. Successful businesses tend to start small with minimal fixed costs.

Keeping an eye on the cash flow is mainly about planning ahead so that you know when you will need money to pay for office space, your own and perhaps other people's salary, and future investments.

The key here is to conduct a liquidity budget. This involves very simple math – plus and minus – but the tricky thing is to include every little probable item. For instance, you must not forget about expenses to the income tax or VAT authorities – money that you may well get back in a year, but money you still don't have today.

Start out with three scenarios: one good, one normal, one worst case. The best case will show what opportunities you can (and perhaps should) grasp if you will have the chance. Regarding the worst-case scenario: if you will make it through this one, you know that you are well prepared for now.

Don't be frightened of planning for negative cash flow. There often are periods when businesses can be run at a loss, as long as profits or payments are expected to roll in soon. The trick is to calculate for negative cash flow and work out how to deal with it: e.g. organising overdrafts in advance.

Music festivals such as Iceland Airwaves, Hultsfred and Sweden Rock often have to pay for big advances before they can market their headline acts and subsequently sell tickets. Mr. Destiny from Iceland Airwaves says his toughest task is to manage the cash flow. Years of experience have given him confidence that his festival will attract enough visitors, but his business model requires loans, sometimes with high interest rates. He has tried to develop several revenue streams in order to balance his vulnerability to one activity and distribute his revenues on a more stable basis year-around (as seen in Axiom 4).

There are many ways in which cash flow can be managed. The trick is to be constantly aware of exactly how you are doing and to plan for what is likely to happen in the short term.

CASE: MR. DESTINY
CONCERT PROMOTIONS AND
THE ICELAND AIRWAVES MUSIC FESTIVAL.
REYKJAVIK, ICELAND.

Artistic productions, fashion collections, or music festivals are usually fixed cost productions, where the cost is typically incurred long before you know whether the product is going to be a hit or not. This can cause serious cash flow problems that are difficult to solve given the uncertain future of the product. Added to this many creative industries products are long range projects, sometimes taking years to come to fruition or become popular (e.g. books, films, albums) making the cash flow even more difficult to manage and hard to judge.

Thorsteinn Stephensen, owner and manager of Mr. Destiny, had a dream about an international music festival in Reykjavik for a long time. At the same time he thought it was a rather farfetched dream and was sure that the obstacles were insurmountable. One key obstacle to having an international festival in Iceland – its distance from even its nearest neighbours – suddenly got smaller when the airline Icelandair cut a sponsorship deal with a rising Icelandic band, GusGus, opening up a new set of possibilities and investors. The contract gave GusGus some free plane tickets and thus allowed them to pursue their career abroad. Thorsteinn saw this contract as an example of how he could get help to make the dream of an international music festival come true.

The result was Iceland Airwaves, an acclaimed indie festival with a reputation for finding new and upcoming artists from abroad as well as giving Icelandic bands the opportunity to play for the international music press.

The first few years of running Iceland Airwaves were not easy. Although Thorsteinn worked on the project for free, in the first year the main sponsor, Icelandair, had to pick up the pieces and save the project from bankruptcy. All in all, the project required huge investments on behalf of Mr. Destiny and Icelandair.

The festival has now become quite well known and is consistently sold out each year. This makes it possible to better plan the finances:

> "Most of the uncertainties have been eliminated from the model; we know the festival has been sold out the last four years, we know what the tickets sales will bring and thus how much we can spend."

Still it is an expensive venture and the cash in question is not just Icelandic Kronas but also the pounds, dollars and Euros that artists want payment in. With an international event even seemingly easy to calculate costs are seeded with uncertainty as currencies go up and down.

More pressing to the festival's cash questions than shifts in exchange rates, however, are the effects of what is happening in the music industry in general. Since sales of recorded music have plummeted live performance is no longer thought of by record companies or artists as largely promotional touring. Performance is now a revenue stream taken very seriously by artists looking to profit from their music. This then means that artists are asking for increasingly higher amounts for their participation in festivals and being much more careful about the terms and conditions under which they perform. But how, if the Iceland Airwaves festival barely breaks even, does Mr. Destiny survive?

The answer is in hosting more general concerts. In the period of 12 months from 2006 – 2007 Mr. Destiny organised 24 concerts in Iceland. By having a constant stream of smaller events managing cash flow becomes easier since they have resources other than those involved by the big annual festival. The Icelandic market is small and the cost of bringing international artists to Iceland is high. This makes it impossible to have a concert every week, meaning that each and every concert has to make profit. But Thorsteinn says he has been lucky and concerts he had not been expecting to break even on – such as a Nick Cave concert they organised purely because he wanted to – have been successes. The same, however, cannot be said about a concert he planned just because he thought it would make money – he now only puts his money into projects he himself enjoys.

"But yes," he says, "The cash flow is very hard to mange and expensive! The interest rates on an overdraft are very high" He concludes "I would not recommend this to anyone who wants to live a normal life. But of course it's better than anything, the best thing you have ever done. You are organising concerts; live music is what it is all about in my mind."

AXIOM 10:
CASH IS KING

LESSONS

- THOUGH CASH FLOW IS VITAL, MONEY COMES IN MANY FORMS, EACH WITH ITS OWN PLUSES AND MINUSES.

- CREATING PARTNERSHIPS MAY SAVE YOU CASH. FOR INSTANCE, DEALS WHERE YOU SHARE THE RISK AND SPLIT THE REVENUES WITH SUPPLIERS.

- ASK FOR CREDIT. THEN YOU CAN PAY WHEN YOU HAVE THE MONEY, NOT BEFORE (REMEMBER, YOU CAN ALWAYS ASK).

- A WAY TO FINANCE THE FIRST STEPS OF YOUR BUSINESS IS TO WORK PART-TIME, FOR INSTANCE WORKING ON ASSIGNMENT. BUT DON'T END UP AS A CONSULTANT IF THIS IS NOT WHAT YOU STRIVE FOR.

- YOU CAN GET FINANCE THROUGH LOANS OR SELLING SHARES OF YOUR COMPANY EQUITY. THIS CAN BE ACHIEVED, EITHER THROUGH PROFESSIONAL FINANCIAL INVESTORS AND BANKS OR THROUGH FRIENDS.

- BE CAREFUL ABOUT SELLING EQUITY. AT LEAST, DON'T SELL IT TO THE WRONG PERSON OR FOR THE WRONG PRICE.

MONEY IS NOT JUST MONEY

OTHER MONEY

Money comes in many different forms. You can get if from the bank, from an investor, win the lottery, or dig into your own savings.

You can also create partnerships and work closely with clients, subcontractors and other companies. Interdependence can create magic.

With suppliers and contractors there are a few opportunities. One is to simply ask for extra credit time. The supplier may say yes to this with the prospects of or guarantee that you will become a long-term customer.

Extra credit time may also be a good option in your own business model. This is an important part of how the fashion company Odd Molly is organized. Money goes out at the same time that money comes in. The suppliers offer credit time until the clothes are delivered, matching the credit time Odd Molly's customers have received.

Another way is to aim to generate extra money for your supplier in a partnership. You have the idea and the concept, but the supplier has the raw materials. In this case, the supplier gets a share of the sales; usually a share greater than the unit price if you had paid up front.

Another model of course is a combination. You pay a low fixed price, but also a share of the revenues. You can also let the supplier get more closely involved than that. One of Odd Molly's main shareholders is actually one of their suppliers.

Yet another model is to create a new company with a partner. This may be a good idea if the partner knows something you don't, for instance regarding local conditions.

Ask yourself too if other organizations want to ally themselves with you. There may be many reasons why another company would consider a partnership with you very useful or profitable.

- The rock festivals Sweden Rock and Hultsfred get a good price for the beer they sell since they give exclusive rights for one supplier, who in turn gets publicity as well as a captive market.

– Mr. Destiny created a partnership with Icelandair in order to get free or reduced plane tickets, the airline got valuable publicity and an event that might help support tourism to their main market.

– The Norwegian café and cultural arena Pavilion received financing thanks to the bank Cultura who wanted to develop its ethical and cultural profile.

Another way of keeping your business going with low costs is to avoid paying a salary to yourself. Not budgeting for a paycheck, however, is not viable in the long run: that would prove something is seriously wrong with your business. Nonetheless, this may be necessary in the beginning. An option is to make money separately for that purpose.

– The founders of the Swedish fashion company Whyred worked part-time for other companies before focusing wholeheartedly on their own. They tried to avoid conflicts of interest and to some degree worked under their own name, building their own brand while designing specific collections for other companies.

The risk with many of these ways of cross subsidising your business through extra jobs and partnerships is that you may end up with another business, namely a consulting business, which maybe was not what you planned for in the beginning. Nothing wrong with that, but if you want to stick to your original plan you have to make room for it and eventually let go.

LOANS OR INVESTMENTS

Maybe you still need more money to finance your business. There are basically three options.

The bank
There is a general view that small and especially creative enterprises have problems getting financing from banks. Our study shows, however, that basically all of them have eventually succeeded with this. The solution for most of them has lain in how they have presented their business. The success formula includes being brief and realistic and having thought about your business model, not only your product.

Be aware that what one bank will offer can be completely different from other alternatives. For instance, switching banks led to much better terms for Dnmark.

There are also state-owned banks which may be less risk averse since they are under orders to encourage new businesses. A few of the companies we have met have taken advantage of such opportunities.

Family and friends
If family and friends know your strengths and notice your dedication, then they may be willing to invest or to lend you money. Families in particular are a key source of finance and advice for many businesses.

The Swedish association Rockparty prefers to borrow from friends and acquaintances instead of from the bank in order to save time and avoid hassle. The association also partly financed its restaurant through selling low priced shares to lots of people.

The downside with this model is of course that you put personal relationships at stake if something goes wrong.

Professional investors
A third alternative for getting more money is to get financing by selling a share of your company to investors: that is selling equity or convertible debt to professional investors.

For the most part professional investors, such as venture capital firms or 'business angels' (wealthy private investors), first enter a new business when it has a proven business model and has reached a certain level of turnover (often around 1 million Euros). Some don't enter new businesses unless the founder has a track-record of starting successful businesses.

How do you find an investor? It varies greatly between industries: e.g. venture capital firms in the IT industry are very different from those found in the film industry.

Some general rules apply: Read the trade papers and magazines and look for names and companies. Contact agencies and trade organizations that act as intermediaries. Ask around in your network. And if you don't have one – well it is time to leave your office or production space and meet some new people.

WHAT IS BEST?

If you do not have the money yourself and need to get it from someone else, what is best? Should you strive for partnership with investors? Should you get a bank loan? Should you call your friends?

It is up to you. The different options have pros and cons. Money is not just money, since different sources of financing bring different conditions and terms and possibilities.

Still, a conclusion from our study is that the entrepreneurs we have talked to all advise against selling equity in the very early stages.

Many have nonetheless valued dedicated and experienced partners, whereas a few of them have regrets that they sold out to professional investors. The lines between partners and investors will always be blurred so it is important to think of the terms as being very similar and to treat each new input – even if at face value it is only money or finance – with due diligence.

This goes back to the discussion of finding the right partner (Axiom 3). Christian Wåhlberg, CEO of the music production company Murlyn, tells a story about good and bad partners and how he has lost a lot of money and energy by being involved with in bad partnerships. Nevertheless, he celebrates his current partner and the major shareholder in Murlyn, the venture capital firm Novax, which he says has given him continuous strategic advice.

Jan Carl Adelswärd, previously CEO of Novax and currently CEO of Filippa K, says that being interested in the industry is as important for the investor as it is to investee: "If you invest in sawdust you better love sawdust." Thus be sure to partner with an investor who knows the industry and can do a good job as an active owner, strategy-wise. Be sure that they share similar interests and that their ideas for the future and their exit strategies (e.g. when and what will make them leave) are similar to those you are interested in.

Conflicts of interest with investors can spiral into open disputes and battles for control. The fashion company J. Lindeberg has been shaken by internal conflicts for several years. The disagreements accelerated in 2007, when the CEO, Arnt Jakobsen, sent an e-mail to the founder, Johan Lindeberg. The e-mail later became public:

> "Michelangelo had to obey the Pope. You have to take orders from your shareholders."

Johan Lindeberg started his company in 1997 and his analysis is that he lost his ownership too early, having had too big ambitions too early and therefore an urgent and constant need for capital.

> "The conflict actually started already in 1998 when I became dependent on investors. There has since then been a frustration from both sides."*

Perhaps you don't need so much money to begin with. If you can navigate and still move forward perhaps professional investors or a big bank loan will not be needed. The fashion company Odd Molly started out with about 150,000 Euros. Six years after the company was founded it generates almost 25,7 million Euros in revenues. Co-founder Christer Andersson says it was fortunate that they did not have so much money at the start. Thanks to that, they were able to keep the majority of the company and steer it in the direction they wanted.

---

* Neither Johan Lindeberg nor Arnt Jakobsen have been interviewed for this study. The text refers to Leopold, Linda, "Kreatören & Kapitalet," Bon, nr 41, 2007.

CASE: PAVILION
ARTS AND CULTURE ARENA AND CAFÉ.
OSLO, NORWAY.

Pavilion is a café and a cultural scene in the Grünerløkka district of Oslo. It is a company based around a special building owned by the Oslo municipality and though their main revenue is from the café, they have art exhibitions and a stage for concerts. After a long process, Hugo Hansen and his two business partners won the lease for the building, which used to be an industrial building for gas heating. At the time they took over the premises, the house was in such a poor state that it was considered a risk for the public but gradually it was renovated to the extent that it has received architectural awards for renovation.

The story starts with Hugo's job in the culture department of the local municipality. From his work at the municipality he knew the building and that a different department in the municipality had decided something needed to be done with the building. With his partners and with his experience of the municipality a company was formed and a long negotiation process was embarked upon.

It soon became apparent that the key problem was that they needed a lot of money, not just to start a company but to renovate a sensitive old industrial building. Investing in building projects such as this one is something that few venture capitalists get involved with so Hansen's only real option was to approach banks.

However, they soon found that not all banks are the same. Hugo went to most of the main Norwegian banks and though they were free to take out personal loans none of the banks was interested in financing the project as a business loan. He says:

"We went to all the ordinary banks and financing institutions. At three of them we got past the first desk clerk but were turned down at the next level in the hierarchy. At Cultura we got a yes after the first meeting."

Cultura Bank is the main financier of the project and contributed about 75% of the start-up costs; the rest of the money came from the loans and savings of the three partners. Cultura Bank is a so called ethical bank which means that they guarantee that their investments and loans will be used in accordance with high social, human rights and/or environmental standards.

At the first meeting they were accepted at once. The reason for this was the bank's social and ethical profile, which meant that they were attracted to a cultural project like this.

"Our profile as a cultural meeting point fits with Cultura's profile – neither of us has profit maximising as the main goal. Rather, we want to contribute to the society."

This does not mean that Cultura is not a bank and it would not finance commercially unsound projects. Pavilion therefore needed to be explained and detailed in a sound business plan. However, dealing with an ethical bank brought with it very different conditions and costs from those usually found in the banking world. Cultura has a sliding interest rate that depends on the project's ethical and/or environmental profile. Pavilion came out high on this scale which meant that they pay relatively high interest rates. Hansen thinks that now that they are established they could get lower rates if they re-financed at another bank but he is loyal to Cultura since they acted nicely in the initial stages. Pavilion has even bought stocks in the bank.

The project is now up and running and managed to break-even in its first year. Despite this Hugo is keen to keep costs down and invested a lot of time in the project without taking out much of a salary. The initial marketing was word-of-mouth because they could not afford a full marketing campaign. Exhibitors and musicians who use the space help out with art, design, printing, and publicity. Apart from the café, which is meant to be the income generator, much of the space is given away for free to cultural activities. Whether it is an art exhibit or a rock musical event, nobody pays money to exhibit or play there.

CASE: FUNCOM
COMPUTER AND CONSOLE GAMES DEVELOPER
AND PUBLISHER.
OSLO, NORWAY.

Computer and console games are enormously capital intensive projects that take teams of highly specialized labour working long hours to complete. Financing is one of the most central issues any business interested in gaming now faces. However, the Norwegian company Funcom has managed to find the right sort of money.

Funcom was started in 1993 and focuses on developing action adventure computer games and Massively Multiplayer Online Role-Playing Games (MMORG). Since its start it has rapidly expanded and has released over 25 games, including Dreamfall and Anarchy Online. In 2008 they released the MMORG 'The Age of Conan,' which became one of the fastest selling PC games ever after selling more than 400,000 copies in its first week.

The company has changed form considerably since it started as "development for hire." Making games for others did not suit the company's ambitions and they decided to start to develop and market their own games. They saw the market potential in online gaming early, and in 2001 launched the game 'Anarchy Online' (AO). This was a difficult time economically and represented a turning point for the company.

They restructured their organisation to be more professional and streamlined. They got a new CEO who reorganised the company to cut costs and had to lay off workers. AO was launched and became a commercial hit; indeed it is still making money. This showed potential investors that the firm could handle costs and produce commercially viable games. In order to further expand they needed money and planned to raise it by going public. They went to financiers and venture capitalists who for a share in the company invested in them and helped them go public. An Initial Public Offering (IPO) was launched in 2005 and the stock is now listed on the Oslo Stock Exchange.

Olav Sandnes says that: I think the investors look at three factors before they invest:

- How is the market developing – this is growing for the gaming industry. Especially Massive Multiplayer Online games because they cannot be copied.
- Is there a working business model?
- What is this company's producing competence, or can they deliver a quality product?

In particular the business model behind online games is attractive to investors. Gamers buy the game and then sign up for a monthly subscription package that allows them to play online. For the big MMOGs the average subscription time is between 6 to 18 months. In addition, games often have periodic 'expansion packs' with new features or scenarios which players can buy. This model is in sharp contrast to that for offline games which are so frequently copied that it is difficult to make money. As Sandnes notes, after their offline game Dreamfall was launched in the shops there were between 200,000 and 300,000 illegal copies downloaded. They decided that this would be the last offline game and that they would concentrate on the online market. Sandnes suggests other cultural businesses can learn from how they have reacted to widespread piracy:

> "We are in an industry where there is a business model that works – this is important for other cultural businesses: to show that this works."

What gaming shares with other cultural businesses is importance of continual innovation – innovation that often takes a lot of time. Investors want an innovative company with an interesting product portfolio.

> "I think this is important for investors to show that we want to develop innovative solutions."

Game development is a high risk project. It takes a long time to develop games, so it is important to have patient investors.

Their biggest project to date, 'The Age of Conan,' cost more than the most expensive Norwegian film ever made and this type of game has a budget of between USD 20 and 30 million. The development of Conan was made possible through capital from the owners, and not only from loans. This is not only due to the amount of finance needed but to the risks involved with investing in one big product that can either be avbig hit or a miss.

The level to which the company's value to investors is linked to expectations for one product can be seen from the share price for their stock. The graph below shows the value of the firm's stock on the Oslo exchange in the past year. Initially, the Conan game was meant to be launched in autumn 2007. This was later postponed and as we can see the company rapidly devalued after it announced the delayed release. However, the announcement of a new release in 2008 and some early reviews started a rapid revaluation of the firm.

Sandnes thinks it is important for the company to be listed on the stock exchange because it makes the company value visible. Two of the three biggest owners are venture capital firms. The owners are mainly foreign, two Scandinavian firms and one Dutch firm. The rest of the owners are smaller, both Norwegian and foreign. These owners know how to invest but they do not know the gaming business. Game development is a new and relatively unstable industry:

"The market views Funcom as a high risk stock."

For Funcom then lots of money has been needed but different types of money had very different time frames and levels of commitment. The early stage venture capitalists and other financers had a very different time horizon than the current stock market investors. Different types of money then have very different types of reaction to events within firms: reactions firms have to carefully watch.

CHAPTER 11: THE INVESTORS' PERSPECTIVE

LESSONS

- PUT YOURSELF IN THEIR SHOES: WHAT ARE THEY LOOKING FOR?
- PLAN FOR THEIR QUESTIONS AND ADDRESS THEIR CONCERNS

As we have seen investors come in many forms and have many different interests and motivations – different investors will be looking for different things. Banks and building societies will be looking for security and the ability to pay back a scheduled loan. Venture capitalists are often looking for the next big thing; something with the possibility of becoming enormous and generating lots of money. Thus banks might be looking very closely at you as an individual: what debts do you have? Do you own something of value? Venture capitalists, in contrast, are seldom investing in individuals but rather in ideas and intellectual property that can be scaled up. For a venture capitalist then it is important that the project can still work even if you walk in front of a car tomorrow or if they decide they need to replace you.

Different types of investors thus will evaluate you in different ways. It is important for you to be aware of their different interests and motivations if you decide to approach them. In the rest of this chapter we will look more closely at what some venture capitalists are interested in and what advice they can give to interested parties.

First, a word of warning: venture capital is only one form of financing your business and not suited to all of you. As Heikki Masalin, Managing Director of CIM Creative Industries Management ltd., says the venture capitalist perspective is not always suitable for analyzing small companies. Not all small companies, although profitable, have the potential for the level of success and revenues that venture capitalists are typically interested in. Those ideas that have the potential to comfortably secure the livings of a few people, generally do not match the expectations venture capitalists have for their investments. Smaller scale projects are therefore more suited to financing from traditional banks, angel investors or family and friends.

Although banks do not require the same return on investment as the venture capitalists, they often prove difficult for the small companies. Our research shows that it can be difficult for start-up creative businesses without any history to get loans from banks; at least unless you or someone connected to the company is willing to put up collateral.

The difficulty in getting that first loan from the bank often leads creatives to borrow from family, friends or any 'fool' with a connection to the new enterprise (this group of investors thus sometimes referred to as the 3Fs). These are the people who love and trust you and will support you through everything no matter what, they are also referred to as "emotional investors" and typically do not provide capital on the basis of strictly financial criteria. When choosing this kind of capital for your company you need to keep this in mind; that you have to be very open and honest about the risks and rewards of the project.

There are then, many different ways to get investment in your business and this makes it very hard to summarize 'the' investor's perspective. Nonetheless we want to point out some common themes that emerged from of investigation into the perspective of investors such as venture capitalists and seed financiers:

- Many firms who contact investors have a tendency to think it is the investor's job to see the project as an investment and do not understand that it is their job, not the investor's, to prove how the project will generate sufficient profit to justify the investment.

- Investors do not take the first step unless there is a clear business and revenue model that shows how the project will be successful/profitable. Although investors don't expect every investment to pay off, they are especially careful with business areas they have no experience of or business areas that are relatively new.

- Investors have limited funds and thus have to make hard decisions on what to put money into and what to skip. Rejection of a proposal should not be taken personally – rather potential investees should ask why they were rejected, learn from this, and try again.

- Small entrepreneurs often lack a clear idea of what their exit strategy is; a clear idea of exit strategies (what and when can or will be sold or dumped) is important to investors.

- Smaller start-ups, especially creative companies, have capital needs that place them below the radar of most venture capitalists.

Let's turn then to what some venture capitalists themselves say. Heikki Masalin, suggests that what venture capitalists and equity investors are looking for:

"is to provide equity, foresee the exit mode and expect profits through a rapid increase in the value of the investee."

This means that the investors' focus is not always on the work or products. Rather it is the potential there is for rapid growth. It is important then that you show what types of value or assets your project will generate by itself: value that can be taken on by someone else if you or your team cannot, or do not want to, continue at the helm. As Heikki says:

"Even in the case of well received products and services, and related strong cash flow, the value of the producers or production company will seldom increase that much. This means venture capitalists' concept and expectations are not met. Rather, investors should look to the IPRs which form the assets of interest."

The message then is that investors, such as Heikki, will be extremely interested in the IPR you hold: why it is unique; who is willing to pay for it; and how you can defend it from competition. Getting ready for meetings with such investors means taking careful stock of what it is that your company really owns and the potential these assets have.

Some firms will, of course, find venture capital an attractive option. The large sums needed, for instance, to develop a videogame means that professional investors and funds are an obvious place to look for help.

We asked Mark Johnson, Investment Director at Nordic Venture Partners, to answer some questions about what his venture capital company looks for in a venture and an investee. Below are his answers:

What are the top 5 questions you ask yourself in evaluating potential investees/projects?

1. What is the primary product of the company seeking money? What is important about this product and how is it differentiated? What is the core intellectual property behind this product and how can it be defended?
2. What is the competition in the company's industry segment?
3. What is the market opportunity for the company's product?
4. How much money does the company need? The answer to this question is frequently different than how much the company is asking for.
5. Does this company possess the team to effectively execute its growth strategy?

What are your top 5 turn-ons?

1. Punctuality
2. Appearance
3. Preparedness
4. Professionalism – i.e. no typo's in the presentation
5. Confidence, quality and knowledge. In general, are the people representing the company raising money able to effectively communicate why they are a fantastic investment case in terms of uniqueness, growth potential, and execution ability?

What are your top 5 turn-offs?

1. Being late
2. Being disorganized when presenting the investment case

3. Having to ask 20 minutes into a presentation what it is that the company actually does
4. Asking me to sign an NDA (Non-Disclosure Agreement) at a first meeting
5. Not being able to effectively break down the market need for the product. Of course, it is initially very important to communicate the uniqueness of the technology that has been developed. However, what we are primarily interested in is how this technology can be commercialized, and obviously that is dependent upon consumer demand.

What pieces of advice would you give to people who are about to present their firms at your office?

Prepare a professional presentation that concisely and accurately communicates:

- What the company does. What is special, unique, and inimitable about the company's product and strategy

- What the customer need is for the product

- What the market growth potential is

- How the company will grow to become dominant in its sector, with competitor analysis

- How much money will be needed and for what purpose

- Be on time

- Be relaxed and not-pushy – while not being arrogant. Confidence in achieving your growth ambitions regardless of our participation is much more attractive than appearing desperate.

Much of what both Heikki and Mark point to as being important to investors is echoed by research in other countries. A study into investment in the creative industries in the United Kingdom* suggests that United Kingdom investors found the following points especially crucial when identifying and evaluating investment opportunities:

- The quality and experience of the management team
- Clarity on who the customers are and how to reach them
- The potential to be a market leader
- The ability to establish 'barriers to entry' against potential competition
- Exit strategies must be formulated
- The investor must know the sector well

The message from all the above is that investors have their own perspective and interests that may be different from yours. This does not, however, mean they are uninterested or hostile: quite the opposite. At the end of the day all investors are interested in new projects and possibilities – after all, they rely for their own success on being able to constantly find new investment projects. In short, they may be as interested in meeting you as you are in meeting them.

---

* NESTA (National Endowment for Science, Technology and the Arts) 2006, Creating Value: How the UK can invest in new creative businesses. NESTA: London.

THE AUTHORS

TOBIAS NIELSÉN is the CEO at the research-based consulting and publishing firm Volante QNB based in Stockholm, Sweden. His work focuses on entrepreneurship, innovation and creativity, often involving forecasting, intersections and urban planning. Tobias has been a speaker at conferences in Hong Kong, New York, Beijing and London. Tobias Nielsén has a Master's Degree from studies at Stockholm School of Economics, Sweden, and Columbia Business School in New York City, USA. He has a background as journalist.

DOMINIC POWER is Professor of Economic Geography at Uppsala University in Sweden. His research is concerned with innovation, entrepreneurship and work in the cultural economy and industries: in particular the music, design and fashion industries. Dominic has worked as a policy adviser and consultant to various Nordic and European government ministries and authorities in the areas of cultural, innovation and industrial policy. He has been involved with and advised a number of small but very creative businesses.

MARGRÉT SIGRÚN SIGURÐARDÓTTIR is Assistant Professor at the University of Iceland Business School, where she runs a research centre on the creative industries. Margret also teaches at the Icelandic Art Academy. In her research Margret has focused on creativity and organisation and her PhD from Copenhagen Business School focused on how the conflict between the artistic and commercial logic influences organisation in the recorded UK music industry.

If you want to hire us as speakers, email speakers@volante.se

WWW.CREATIVEBUSINESS.ORG

www.ingramcontent.com/pod-product-compliance
Lightning Source LLC
Chambersburg PA
CBHW020436220526
45464CB00002B/732